EcoManagement

EcoManagement

THE ELMWOOD GUIDE
TO ECOLOGICAL AUDITING
AND SUSTAINABLE BUSINESS

Ernest Callenbach

Fritjof Capra

Lenore Goldman

Rüdiger Lutz

Sandra Marburg

Berrett-Koehler Publishers
San Francisco

Berrett-Koehler Publishers, Inc.
155 Montgomery Street
San Francisco, CA 94104-4109
Tel: 415-288-0260   Fax: 415-362-2512

ORDERING INFORMATION

Individual sales. Berrett-Koehler publications are available through most bookstores. They can also be ordered direct from Berrett-Koehler at the address above.

Quantity sales. Special discounts are available on quantity purchases by corporations, associations and others. For details, contact the "Special Sales Department" at the Berrett-Koehler address above.

Orders for college textbook/course adoption use. Please contact Berrett-Koehler Publishers at the address above.

Orders by U.S. trade bookstores and wholesalers. Please contact Publishers Group West, 4065 Hollis Street, Box 8843, Emeryville, CA 94662; 510-658-3453; 1-800-788-3123.

Printed in the United States of America

Printed on acid-free and recycled paper that meets the strictest state and U.S. guidelines for recycled paper (50 percent recycled waste, including 10 percent postconsumer waste).

This book is printed with vegetable-based inks.

Library of Congress Cataloging-in-Publication Data

EcoManagement: the Elmwood guide to ecological auditing and sustainable business/ by Ernest Callenbach...(et al.)—1st ed.
     p.   cm.

    Includes bibliographical references and index.
    ISBN 1-881052-27-3 (hard : Alk. paper)
1. Industrial management—Environmental aspects—Management
   I. Callenbach, Ernest   II. Elmwood Institute
   HD69.P6E28   1993
   658.4'08—dc20   93-17285
                                                   CIP

First Edition
     First Printing 1993

Cover Design by Mary Sanichas
Book Design and Production by Elizabeth Swenson and Janja Lalich, Book Producers

*For our children and their children's children
who deserve our deepest commitment
to leave them a sustainable earth.*

CONTENTS

PREFACE

This book grew out of an Elmwood Institute project called Global File, which collects, analyzes, and distributes information about successful ecological practices in business and government. In Elmwood's view, the nineties are a critical decade, characterized by a profound change from a mechanistic worldview to an ecological view, from a value system based on domination to one based on partnership. The challenge of the nineties is to create sustainable societies, that is, social and cultural environments in which we can "satisfy our needs without jeopardizing the prospects of future generations" (Brown et al. 1990, 173).

Our first Global File report, "The Development of Ecologically Conscious Management in Germany" (Lutz 1990), focused on Germany, one of the countries in which ecological awareness has progressed furthest among the general public, as well as in business and in politics. It discussed the concept and practice of ecologically conscious management by the German business community as an interesting illustration of what may be expected in other countries in the near future.

The present work carries these concerns forward and focuses on the practice of "ecological auditing" (or "eco-auditing") which is being increasingly recognized as an essential tool of contemporary management. Here we refine and enlarge the conceptual framework of eco-auditing beyond that developed in Germany (and beyond the mainly compliance auditing developed in the United States), and we attempt to set new standards for this rapidly developing field.

This guide does not intend to give detailed directions on how to do an eco-audit. Rather it maps out the cultural and conceptual framework, sets the standard for ecomanagement, and describes the corporate culture required to produce an eco-audit. It also argues that only an audit of such a "deep ecological" nature will truly reduce the environmental impact of a company's operations. Finally, it outlines the dimensions and objectives of an eco-audit and provides general guidance for planning one.

To actually carry out an eco-audit of the kind described and advocated in this book, however, it is necessary to bring in, or identify within the company, auditing teams with various kinds of expertise (energy, chemicals, recycling, and so on). In their planning, these teams should consider using both quantitative and qualitative methods for conducting the audit. To give an idea of what these might be, we present a short menu of them. Some of these methods will be more germane to a given company than to others.

STRUCTURE OF THE BOOK

The book is divided into two parts. Part I (Chapters 1–4) discusses the origin and conceptual framework of ecomanagement. Part II (Chapters 5–11) gives a detailed account of the theory and practice of ecomanagement advocated by the Elmwood Institute.

Chapter 1 reviews the origin of "environmental audits" in Europe and the United States during the 1970s and 1980s, the later shift from a defensive and reactive attitude toward environmental protection to a proactive and creative attitude in German and Swiss companies, business trends toward systemic management, and the principles of ecologically conscious management that resulted from the new creative approaches.

Chapter 2 surveys various methods of environmental data analysis and discusses the problem of quantification and the relevance of values, which are central questions for all environmental auditing and management.

Chapter 3 surveys innovative work being done in a great variety of company settings, describing dramatic improvements in ecological performance. It also lists organizations, in the United States and abroad, that are assisting companies through the process of change.

Chapter 4 introduces Elmwood's distinction between "environmental" and "ecological" management, comparing it to the distinction between "shallow environmentalism" and "deep ecology" coined by Arne Naess (1973) in the 1970s. Environmental management, from our perspective, lacks an ethical dimension, does not question the dominant paradigm, perpetuates the illusion of economics as a value-free science, and subscribes to the ideology of economic growth. Ecological management and auditing, by contrast, is motivated by an ecological ethic. It involves a shift from mechanistic to systemic thinking and from a value system based on domination to one based on partnership. It replaces the ideology of economic growth with that of ecological sustainability. The different values and strategies for ecological change, brought into play by pioneer and mainstream companies, are explored. The links among ecological, social, and diversity issues are discussed.

Chapter 5 deals with the renewing of corporate culture, which is the basis of ecological management. Several aspects of this redefinition (in theory and practice) are discussed in this chapter, from values and thinking to organizational structure and expression.

Chapter 6 introduces the concept of the company as a living system with its internal and external ecology. This chapter contains a generic "metabolic flow chart" developed by the Elmwood Institute as a conceptual aid for comprehensive eco-auditing.

Chapters 7, 8, 9, and 10 apply the metabolic flow chart in a systematic discussion of the practice of eco-auditing. These chapters cover the four major areas of ecomanagement: inflow, processing and manufacturing, outflow, and structures supporting the flow. Each chapter contains several checklists that combine elements developed in Germany with elements from practices elsewhere, plus some new elements developed by the Elmwood Institute.

Chapter 11 describes the eco-auditing sequence and the resulting action plan, and discusses ways to establish priorities. It reiterates the essential point that eco-auditing and ecologically conscious management can only succeed if top management is fully committed to the process and to its continuing implementation.

ACKNOWLEDGMENTS

The authors wish to thank many people who assisted in the preparation of this volume.

Nicole Jordan brought to bear her extensive experience of the business world. Regina Münch carried out invaluable research and helped to bring order to the process of manuscript revisions. James

Warner contributed philosophic clarity to our conceptions. Petra Loesch and Francis Marburg translated many complex documents from the German language. As we were developing the manuscript, Janice Baker and Michael Weil were instrumental in integrating our disparate types of visual and written material into a pleasing whole. Janja Lalich and Elizabeth Swenson provided the final editorial and book production skills, bringing the project to completion.

The preparation of the original manuscript was funded, in part, by a grant from Esprit de Corp.

June 1993   The Elmwood Institute
Berkeley, California

ABOUT THE ELMWOOD INSTITUTE

The Elmwood Institute, founded in 1984 by Fritjof Capra, is an educational institution dedicated to fostering ecological literacy. As defined by the Institute, ecological literacy consists of three components: systems thinking, knowledge of the principles of ecology, and the practice of ecological values. The members of the Institute, an international network of thinkers and activists, share the following perceptions of the present world situation:

The major problems of our time are all systemic problems—interconnected and interdependent. These problems can only be understood and solved if we learn how to think systemically, in terms of relationships, connectedness, and context.

We are destroying our natural environment because of our ignorance of ecology. Being ecologically literate means understanding the principles of ecology, the "language of nature."

Ecological literacy also includes deep ecology, a value system that is earth-centered rather than human-centered, respecting the richness and diversity of all life forms.

The Institute's *EcoManagement Program* explores the terrain in which ecology and business interface. It promotes ecologically conscious management and sustainable business, and encourages the transformation of values, ideas, and behavior through research, education, dialogue, and networking.

For membership information, please call (510) 845-4595; or write to The Elmwood Institute, 2522 San Pablo Avenue, Berkeley, CA 94710; fax (510) 845-1439.

About the Authors

Ernest Callenbach is the author of the ecological classic, *Ecotopia*, which has been translated into ten languages, and of a "prequel," *Ecotopia Emerging*. He also wrote, with Michael Phillips, *A Citizen Legislature*, and, with his wife Christine Leefeldt, a best-selling children's book, *Humphrey the Wayward Whale*. His most recent book is *Living Cheaply with Style*, a guide to living better and with less environmental impact. He lectures all over the world on ecological topics, and is Scholar in Residence at the Elmwood Institute.

Fritjof Capra, physicist and systems theorist, is the founder and president of the Elmwood Institute, an ecological think tank dedicated to fostering ecological literacy. Dr. Capra, who is on the faculty of Schumacher College in England, is engaged in research in systems theory and its applications. He is the author of three international best-sellers, *The Tao of Physics*, *The Turning Point*, and *Uncommon Wisdom*. He coauthored *Green Politics* with Charlene Spretnak and, more recently, *Belonging to the Universe* with David Steindl-Rast. He also cowrote the screenplay for the feature film based on Capra's books, *Mindwalk*, starring Liv Ullman, Sam Waterston, and John Heard.

Lenore Goldman, M.B.A., is an organizational consultant to business, government, and nonprofit organizations in strategic planning, diversity, and ecological change. She specializes in working with organizations that seek to combine their social, environmental, and financial goals. Her clients have included Esprit, Kaiser-Permanente, Nissan-Europe, World Wildlife Fund, Planned Parenthood, Working Assets Common Holdings, and the City of Santa Fe. Ms. Goldman coauthored "Building a Total Quality Culture" in *The Nonprofit Management Handbook*, and the *Strategic Diversity Profile*, an instrument that assesses workplace culture and gender issues.

Based in the San Francisco Bay Area, she has recently been involved in consulting projects in Eastern and Central Europe.

Rüdiger Lutz, born in 1953 in Tübingen, Germany, is a trained architect and psychologist, specializing in ecology and systemic future research. Holding degrees from the University of Berlin and the University of California, Berkeley, he founded several ecological research organizations and conducted hundreds of Future workshops throughout Europe, the United Kingdom, and the United States. He has taught Design Ecology and Planning Theory at universities in Europe and was a professor at the Berlin Academy of Arts. Putting theory into practice, he started ecomanagement as a top manager for a German office furniture manufacturer in the framework of the Elmwood Guide. He has written and edited over a dozen books and hundreds of articles, among them the German edition of this book, *Innovationsökologie,* published in Munich in 1992. He is currently with the Elmwood Institute and lives in the San Francisco Bay Area.

Sandra Marburg has taught environmental studies and geography at several universities and colleges, and is currently a lecturer at the University of California, Berkeley. While conducting environmental research at the U.S. Environmental Protection Agency's National Marine Laboratory, she functioned as the women's program coordinator with the Civil Service Administration, designing policies to promote the careers of women scientists. She has also organized conferences on ecofeminism, coastal pollution, and sustainable global population. Her research areas include American environmental and natural resource history, women's roles in resource use and management, and ecological sustainability.

PART I

THE CONCEPT AND DEVELOPMENT OF ECOMANAGEMENT

1

TRENDS TOWARD ECOLOGICALLY CONSCIOUS MANAGEMENT

During the 1970s and 1980s the environmental disasters of Seveso, Bhopal, Chernobyl, and Basel led to a dramatic rise of environmental awareness throughout Europe, followed by an equally dramatic rise in the United States, where the Valdez oil spill infuriated the general public. Millions of people around the globe came together on Earth Day 1990 to symbolize efforts to "save" the Earth. Today there is widespread agreement that the nineties will be the decade of the environment.

It is important to remember that the environmental damage done by the headlined catastrophes of recent years is small compared to the mostly unnoticed cumulative damage done by vast numbers of smaller polluters, most of them complying with the legal norms of their countries (Winter et al. 1987, 11). In West Germany, for example, the annual environmental damage has been estimated (Wicke 1986, cited in Winter et al. 1987, 17) as follows:

3

Air pollution	Over 48 billion DM ($27 billion)
Water pollution	Well over 18 billion DM ($10 billion)
Soil damage	Well over 5 billion DM ($3 billion)
Noise	Over 33 billion DM ($18 billion)

Total Damage	Well over 104 billion DM ($58 billion)

The overall figure of 104 billion DM represented approximately 6 percent of the West German Gross National Product (GNP) in 1984. No similar "ecological balance sheets" are available for other European countries, but the total environmental damage in these countries has been estimated by the Organization for Economic Cooperation and Development (OECD) at between 3 percent and 5 percent of each country's GNP.

Naturally, these estimates ignore a number of factors, either because they cannot be quantified and monetarized, or because the relevant ecological interdependencies are still unknown. It is likely that the true ecological damage is far greater than present estimates. German unification and the open borders between Western Europe and the former communist bloc have intensified international awareness of environmental damage that is more profound than imagined. The high cost of cleanup remains beyond the reach of Central and Eastern Europe and the Commonwealth of Independent States, and beyond the will of most international businesses, lenders, and investors.

INCREASE IN ENVIRONMENTAL CONCERNS

Beginning in the 1980s, the awareness that "everyday" damages to the environment could be reduced substantially by ecologically sound business practices spread rapidly in many European countries. West Germany, in particular, saw a boom in "eco-friendly" products and services. The strong response of many elements in the West German corporate community to the environmental challenge must be understood against the background of three developments that shaped the German political landscape during the 1980s. These are:

- The rapid increase of environmental awareness in the general public, which had a significant effect on consumer preferences, along with the rise of a powerful ecology movement

- The emergence of technological protest, directed especially against nuclear power and other megatechnologies, as a new form of political protest

- The rise of the Green Party and its successes in introducing critical ecological issues into the political dialogue and the legislative process

These three developments combined to create a business climate in which the perceptions of the environmental dimension of business practices changed significantly in many German companies (Dyllik 1989). Before the 1980s, environmental protection was seen as a very unwelcome, costly side issue that had to be avoided; usually opponents argued that it would diminish a company's competitive edge. This reaction was defensive; its goal was to belittle, fend off, fight, or avoid all claims for environmental damage.

In the 1980s, however, expenses for environmental protection began to be seen by leading companies not primarily as costs but rather as investments in the future and, paradoxically, as a competitive advantage. The defensive, reactive attitude changed into a proactive and creative one. (Figure 1 below illustrates the motivations encouraging businesses to accept responsibility for environmental protection.) "Ecologically conscious management" became the new catch phrase among forward-looking entrepreneurs (Lutz 1990).

With this dramatic shift, some German companies and the German ecology movement began a novel alliance. Because of their available experts, access to both national and local media, and financial resources, industrial firms were able to put into practice many "eco-tech" projects that had been conceived by environmental groups. Thus, the initial antagonism between the grass-roots ecology movement and the corporate world often turned into highly productive cooperation.

The change of perception among German business leaders is well documented by opinion polls. As early as 1984, a survey of the

Fig. 1. Motivation for Environmental Protection in Business

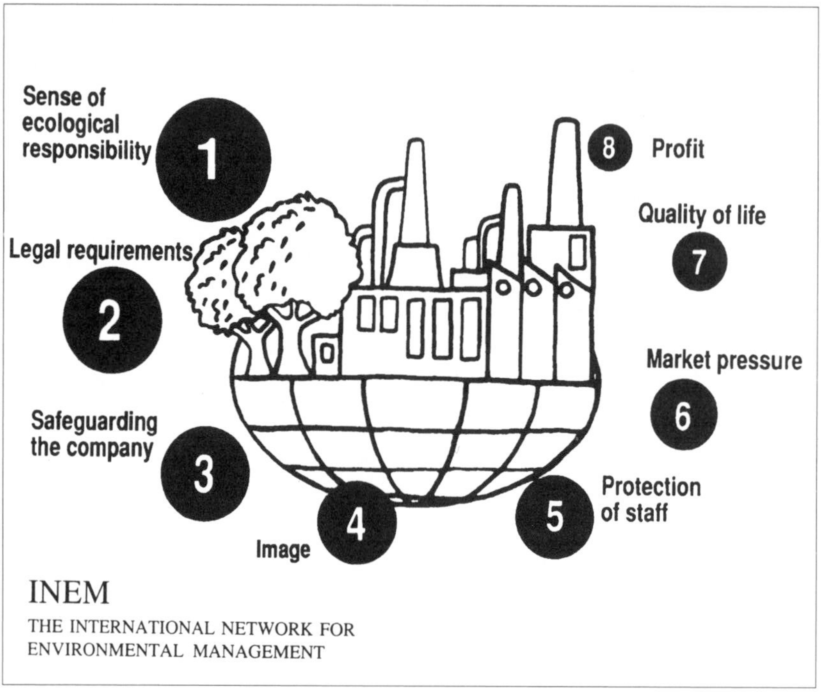

Grafik: © imu - bildinfo, Essen

Association of Young Entrepreneurs found that 77 percent of respondents would welcome the incorporation of environmental protection into the German constitution; 75 percent intended to include more environmental considerations in their production processes, while 60 percent were prepared to make economic sacrifices in the interest of environmental protection (Winter et al. 1987, 21).

In the United States, initiatives by environmentalists to influence business did not rest exclusively on the formation of the Environmental Protection Agency and the unprecedented passage of the Clean Air Act and Clean Water Act in the 1960s. In the 1970s the Conservation Foundation initiated the first collaborative negotiations between environmental advocates and businesses to facilitate more efficient approaches to legislative conflicts. The dialogues served to identify areas of agreement before federal legislation was proposed and to clarify the battle lines. The model for multiparty environmental mediation and collaborative negotiations for the development of environmental regulations was created. This model also served as one alternative to costly litigation.

In the 1980s Americans witnessed the erosion of environmental cleanup, program funding, and legal enforcement against industrial polluters. Federal tax credits for the development of solar and other alternative energy were rescinded. By the end of the decade, Japan and Germany had displaced the U.S.'s leadership on solar energy development by both investment dollars and percentage of their respective national budgets (Piasecki and Asmus 1990). Concurrently, pioneer companies began successfully using environmental approaches to save money and expand sales. The argument that damaging the environment could sabotage corporate competitiveness began gaining credibility.

The 1980s also saw the rise of environmental activism ranging from Earth First! to broad coalitions seeking stricter state environmental legislation. Socially or environmentally screened investment accounted for $625 billion by 1991 (Harrington 1992); environmental screens have been the fastest growing sector by far.

Environmental groups began successful experiments to affect corporate policy. After activists boycotted Burger King, the fast-food chain, for destroying the Brazilian rain forest in order to expand beef production, the Environmental Defense Fund worked with the corporate giant to help reduce styrofoam use and launch major recycling programs. Cultural Survival began importing products from indigenous peoples in endangered habitats, products that are available only through environmental preservation. Nuts and oils from Brazilian rain forests used for the manufacture of food, buttons, and cosmetics constituted the largest portion of Cultural Survival's nearly $30 million in product sales in 1991 to companies like Ben & Jerry's Ice Cream and the Body Shop.

A proliferation of environmentally oriented companies sprouted, from home recycling bin manufacturers to "green" product specialty stores and direct-mail firms. Companies that pioneered socially and environmentally conscious practices began forming associations like the Social Investment Forum, the Social Venture Network, and regional business environmentalist groups. Mainstream companies initiated recycling, carpooling, and energy-efficiency programs.

Long-term strategists began quietly incorporating environmental criteria in acquisition recommendations. As the Cold War ended, national weapons laboratories explored options in hazardous waste cleanup and energy research.

By the time of the second Earth Day in 1990, environmental concerns were also seen to have a dramatic effect on consumer choices in the United States. In a survey taken in April 1990 by the Opinion Research Corporation (McLeod 1990), 71 percent of those surveyed said they had switched brands because of environmental concerns, while 27 percent said they had boycotted products because of a manufacturer's poor environmental record. We can expect that in the United States, too, more and more entrepreneurs will read the signs of the time and embrace the principles of ecologically conscious management.

BUSINESS TRENDS TOWARD SYSTEMIC MANAGEMENT

Several trends in American business have also paved the way toward a more holistic approach to management and organizational change, which is often the vehicle for mainstream companies to incorporate ecological management concerns. These trends offer a related frame of reference and can provide bridge language and currently existing structures in order to introduce environmental concerns into the heart of a business, rather than solely through an add-on program.

Stakeholder Management

To meet the pressures from consumer, community, and interest-group challenges mounted in the 1960s and 1970s, companies began to use the stakeholder management model. Instead of seeing a business as an isolated entity, the business was seen in relationship to a wide range of stakeholders, that is, groups with a stake in the company's actions.

Obvious stakeholders include employees, management, shareholders, and the board of directors. Customers, labor unions, suppliers, vendors, advertisers, and even competitors can be considered stakeholders. Government regulators, the media, citizens of the community in which the company operates, providers of raw materials or components, related industries (such as those who make the ink for the product's packaging), trade associations, other community businesses (who might lose sales if there's a layoff), local hospitals that serve victims of workplace injuries, those served by the nonprofits who receive corporate charitable donations—all have a stake in company operations and may affect or be affected by company choices.

Mapping a business's stakeholders can both expand the recognition of interconnections and spotlight previously unconsidered areas of corporate responsibility. The process can do more than anticipate and prevent unwanted risk. It can suggest new opportunities for partnership and establish a framework for actual face-to-face dialogue to develop joint approaches to corporate problems that may have an impact on stakeholders. Unfortunately, the latter practice is rare among companies. The environment, in fact, can be considered a critical stakeholder in its own right, most often spoken for by environmental advocates. While the connection is obvious for agribusiness or the waste disposal industry, it requires ecological analysis to use the stakeholder model to illustrate the connection for a garment or furniture company.

The stakeholder management approach provides a conceptual tool so that managers can anticipate the impact of outside groups on the company. Risk management departments find this kind of analysis can help prevent problems, particularly from the impact of social protest. It cuts down on surprises. However, stakeholder management is a conceptual framework that provides neither a prescription for action nor a values framework to guide corporate direction.

Total Quality Management

Total Quality Management for the Environment is now being explored in several companies (with Xerox Corporation as one notable example), representing an extension of the Total Quality Management (TQM) movement. Built on work dating back to the 1920s, TQM was developed by W. Edwards Deming after World War II in his work with Japanese companies. The movement was then furthered by Genichi Taguchi, Joseph Juran, Philip Crosby, and others as it gained widespread corporate acceptance in the Western world by the early 1980s (Gabor 1990). Total Quality Management focuses on continuous improvement of business processes in order to more fully meet customer needs and expectations. The strategy was seen as a critical factor in Japan's ability to win market share, sales, profits, and customer loyalty from U.S. and European corporations.

TQM uses an interdependent view of management that reaches well beyond the boundary of the organization. It moves beyond mere end-of-process quality improvement, emphasizing a long-term commitment. The entire system—from initial organization of work teams to customer evaluations long after purchase—is restructured. TQM employs a cooperative team approach, placing the responsibility on management to provide optimal conditions for teams. It emphasizes high employee involvement, decentralization, and multilateral communication—top-down, bottom-up, laterally, or cross-departmentally (Champoux and Goldman 1992).

Total Quality Management and TQM for the Environment can be a useful structure in which to foster ecological awareness, leading to an ecological evaluation of products and processes, as well as an assessment of intrinsic quality and customer service. However, TQM has been under scrutiny for creating relentlessly high-stress working conditions in the continuous pursuit of ever-greater quality. Complex structures to implement the efforts meet with varied success. The emphasis on meeting immediate customer needs can interfere with the creation of new products, the dropping of popular but ecologically unsound products, and proactive consumer education about new environmental products.

Integrating Work, Family, and Life-Style

Companies are also expanding their responsibilities for the internal social environment provided for their employees. As baby boomers began raising families, as more women assumed corporate management positions, and as more male executives found themselves sharing custody of their children after divorce, pressure on companies to accommodate family concerns increased. Even before passage of the federal family leave law in 1993, hundreds of corporations had begun to provide maternity and paternity leave, child care, flextime, job sharing, and discretionary personal/sick leave to reduce the pressures working parents face.

As with improvements in company environmental performance, the favorable results on employee satisfaction, morale, and company loyalty have often been reinforced by actual improvements in work performance. The positive response to such policies has challenged the concept of the isolated individual rising a ladder of individual success at enormous personal cost. The capacity to integrate work and family responsibilities encourages the promotion of women to key corporate positions and the active participation of men in their children's upbringing.

Acknowledgment and support of alternative family structures is beginning, through provision of family, health, bereavement, and other benefits to "domestic partners," including gays, lesbians, and, in some cases, heterosexual couples who choose not to marry. New York's weekly *Village Voice* has provided health benefits to domestic partners since 1982 with no significant change in policy costs resulting from claims. Half of their enrollees are homosexual. The Lotus software company provides such benefits to gay and lesbian employees only because they "do not have the choice to legalize permanent and exclusive relationships through marriage" (Mickens 1991, 14).

Since the mid to late 1970s, corporations have been encouraging preventive health practices and healthier life-styles to reduce health insurance costs and improve employee productivity. Health club memberships, on-site gyms or fitness classes, and support groups to help employees lose weight and stop smoking are no longer uncommon.

Many corporations have financed employee drug and alcohol rehabilitation, discovering that it can be less costly to assist in an employee's recovery than to fire and rehire. The social impact is large. The step is also critical to a systemic management perspective, to recognizing and responding to the web of human relationships of which the company is part.

The Learning Organization

Strategies for organizational change historically relied on the premise that one could approach change in a linear, step-by-step fashion. By the mid-1980s, turbulent change had become a way of life for corporations in many industries. Economic instability during the heyday of leveraged buyouts and junk bonds only exacerbated trends toward volatility caused by economic globalization, intensified competition from Japan and Germany, and the acceleration of technological development. How do you operate in a company that faces "permanent white water" (Vaill 1989), in which turbulent, unpredictable change is the norm?

Peter Senge (1990) argues that the organizations that survive and thrive will be those oriented toward the future—able to take in new information, adapt, and change. In essence, to learn. There aren't clear answers for many of the challenges facing companies. Senge believes that organizational success lies in the ability of the group and the individuals within it to incorporate five technologies: systems thinking, personal mastery, mental models, building shared vision, and team learning. These skills enable a team to anticipate and respond to rapidly changing conditions.

It is often to the company's advantage to foster learning among loyal, capable staff rather than constantly fire and rehire as priorities change—or cling to control by denying the need for change. Top management is responsible for creating an organization that fosters learning: asking "dumb" questions, getting support, encouraging experimentation.

ECOLOGICALLY CONSCIOUS MANAGEMENT

To include environmental protection among management goals substantially enlarges the entire conception of management. The goals of management, traditionally, were almost exclusively economic. But since World War II, with the increasing integration of the social dimension into economics, especially in Europe, social goals—job protection, social security, worker participation, humane working conditions, and so forth—were added to the purely economic goals. By the mid-1950s this had resulted in a significant extension of the conception of management, both in theory and in practice (Dyllik 1989).

In the United States, social concerns advocated by the labor movement of the 1930s were eroded in the same post-World War II period under McCarthyism. Organized labor bureaucratized, opting for wage security at the expense of issues related to workers' control; this shift was symbolized by the signing of the first three-year contract by the United Auto Workers in 1950. The subsequent rise in real wages and job security for working Americans coincided with the development of the advertising industry and consumerism. Without a social democratic tradition and an established role of labor in government, such as existed in Europe, millions in the "other" America lived in poverty, without health care or social safety nets. It was not until the legislation brought about by the "Great Society" and the social movements of the 1960s and 1970s that the discontinuity of social reform was challenged. In the eighties, however, important socioeconomic and environmental achievements were again dismantled or languished unenforced.

Germany's development was more consistent. During the 1980s, in many quarters the German conception of management was gradually extended to include the ecological dimension. At first, this happened sporadically when individual managers and entrepreneurs started recycling programs, energy-saving measures, and other ecological innovations in their companies. These practices spread rapidly, and soon several business pioneers developed comprehensive, ecologically oriented systems of management.

The most successful of these comprehensive systems has been the "integrated system of ecologically conscious management" developed by Georg Winter, known today simply as the "Winter model." On the practical side, several companies joined forces to form the Federal Association for Ecologically Conscious Management (German acronym BAUM, meaning "tree"), for the purpose of promoting and refining the Winter model (see Lutz 1990).

BENEFITS OF ECOLOGICALLY CONSCIOUS MANAGEMENT

Winter lists six reasons why any responsible manager or entrepreneur should implement the principles of ecologically conscious management in his or her company (Winter et al. 1987, 21):

1. *Human survival:* without ecologically conscious companies, we cannot achieve an ecologically conscious economy; without an ecologically conscious economy, human survival will be endangered.

2. *Public consensus:* without ecologically conscious companies, there will be no public consensus with the business community; without such consensus, the market economy would be in political jeopardy.

3. *Market opportunities:* without ecologically conscious management, there will be a loss of fast-growing market opportunities.

4. *Reduction of risks:* without ecologically conscious management, companies face risks of liability for environmental damages, potentially involving enormous sums of money and personal liabilities of directors, executives, and other staff members.

5. *Reduction of costs:* without ecologically conscious management, there will be a loss of numerous opportunities for cost reductions.

6. *Personal integrity:* without ecologically conscious management, both managers and employees will sense a lack of personal integrity and thus be unable to fully identify with their jobs.

Job satisfaction is bound to be enhanced with the awareness that one's work is being done with minimal expense to the environment, personal health, and the opportunities of future generations. Lawler's (1969; see also Hackman and Oldham 1980) work on job design has verified that a key component to job context satisfaction is a sense of accomplishment. Organizational transformation theory suggests a similar need for greater meaning and for recognition of the "spiritual" needs of employees. That search for wholeness in relationship to the larger environment is consistent with ecomanagement.

Implicit in this philosophy is the notion of sustainability, which has also become a key concept of the environmental movement in the United States (Brown 1981). Sustainability has also become a buzzword in international business circles since Swiss billionaire Stephan Schmidheiny's Business Council for Sustainable Development (1992) released a plea for corporate environmental commitment coinciding with the UNCED Earth Summit in Rio de Janeiro.

In the Winter model, there are six principles that are considered essential for the long-term success of a responsibly managed company (Winter et al. 1987, 22):

Quality: a product is of high quality only if it is manufactured in an environmentally benign way and if it can be used and disposed of without causing environmental damage. [In Elmwood's view, this formulation is somewhat naive, since all industrial activity causes environmental damage; the objective is to *minimize* damage.]

Creativity: the creativity of the company's work force is enhanced by working conditions that respect human biological needs (low noise, healthy food, ecologically oriented architecture, etc.).

Humaneness: the general working atmosphere will be more humane if the corporate goals and strategies are geared not only toward economic success but also toward a sense of responsibility with regard to all forms of life.

Profitability: the company's profitability can be increased by adopting cost-reducing ecological innovations and by exploiting market opportunities for ecologically appealing products.

Continuity: in the interest of the company's continuity, it is becoming more and more important to avoid liability risks under increasingly stringent environmental legislation and market risks resulting from the decreasing demand for environmentally damaging products.

Loyalty: ultimately, the staff of a company will be loyal to their country and fellow citizens only if they are emotionally attached to it, which will only happen so long as the country has not lost its character through environmental destruction.

The Winter model includes the strategic use of traditional management tools for ecological purposes (Winter et al. 1987, 23). Thus, ecologically oriented managers use the special, often international, channels of communication available to them, as well as their influence in chambers of commerce and professional organizations. The effectiveness of management teams, trained and experienced in setting targets and making sure that they are achieved, is extended to the environmental context. Employee creativity can be mobilized for ecological activities, for example, through employee suggestion schemes.

Three key elements are characteristic of ecologically conscious management strategies (Dyllik 1989). These are:

Innovation: in contrast to traditional capital- and labor-saving innovations, ecologically conscious strategies require "eco-friendly" and resource-conserving innovations. Such ecological innovations may be of two kinds: those reducing the environmental impact of the company's operations, and those bringing the customer ecological advantages. The former will generate cost savings, the latter competitive advantages.

Cooperation: the importance of cooperation among the actors throughout the life cycle of a product—from raw materials through production, use, and disposal—derives from the fact that economic and ecological effects obey different laws. Whereas competition is a guiding principle of the former, cooperation is essential to the latter.

Communication: in traditional management strategies, communication and public relations are understood as components of marketing and restricted to product or image publicity. In ecologically conscious management strategies, by contrast, the task of communication acquires overall strategic importance, due to the crisis of confidence affecting individual companies and entire industries.

2

Methods of Environmental and Ecological Auditing

Ll economic activities have impacts on society and the environment and thus generate social and ecological costs. In conventional economics, no matter how massive these costs may be, they are treated as "externalities." They are excluded from the balance sheets and passed on around the system to the population at large, to the environment, and to future generations (Henderson 1981, 12).

Expansion of "Auditing" beyond Financial Data

In the late 1960s the insulation of business from its real-world context came under heavy criticism in many industrial countries. Following the student and worker revolts in France in 1968 and the black uprisings in Watts, Detroit, and Washington, D.C., the operations of both business and government were subjected to new levels of scrutiny and protest. Informed critics of business, such as Ralph Nader and the Council on Economic Priorities, began to focus public attention on a range of new corporate issues. Most prominent were hiring and promotion of minorities and women; the effects of pollution, product quality, and safety; and community responsibility. The viewpoint spread that a corporation's "constituency" included many other players besides stockholders: employees, consumers, suppliers, communities in which operations were conducted, government, and society as a whole.

By the early 1970s attempts were being made to think about "social accounting"—evaluating the performance of companies on more than simple financial grounds (Bauer 1973). Some of this work was done by business-school analysts, but several American companies developed internal surveys of their performance which were called "social audits." The notion of an "Environmental Exchange Report," using the analogy of cash-flow reports, was also developed (Corcoran and Leininger 1970). In Germany and Switzerland during the late 1970s a similar broadening of the traditional balance sheet took place (Müller-Wenk 1980, cited in Steger 1988, 317).

In the beginning, one social issue was susceptible to quantitative treatment: the hiring, retention, and promotion of minorities and women (later extended to include other categories of workers). Government regulations required corporations to compile yearly numerical reports on their performance in this area, which provided some degree of objective standard for comparison and evaluation.

A few American companies continue to rate themselves on social performance, partly to meet internal management concerns and partly for public relations purposes. The Council on Economic Priorities (CEP) has greatly expanded its work; it now publishes the widely read consumer guide, *Shopping for a Better World* (Marlin, Swaab, and Will 1990). This guide, which is based on extensive questionnaires and direct research, rates companies on charitable giving, women's advancement, minority advancement, defense contracts, animal testing, social disclosure, community outreach, nuclear power, South African involvement, and the environment.

In the sixties, partly in response to Rachel Carson's *Silent*

Spring, a profound change in the American public's attitudes about the need for federal environmental standards put pressure on politicians to act. Pivotal legislation adopted in the late 1960s and early 1970s not only established the Environmental Protection Agency but also set nationwide policies for emissions and discharges, environmental impact assessments, pesticide use, and so forth. With the rise of these national and similar state standards, quantitative assessments of impacts on air, water, toxic levels, and health standards became widespread. These combined developments led to what we term "environmental auditing."

Some American companies have developed internal policies on environmental matters that go beyond the governmental regulatory requirements. The fundamental method in American environmental auditing, however, involves comparing company procedures (in such matters as storage facilities for environmentally hazardous materials or emissions of wastes to air and water) to what is permitted by a complex of laws and regulations. These laws include:

- Clean Air Act
- Clean Water Act
- Resource Conservation and Recovery Act
- Comprehensive Environmental Responsibility, Cleanup, and Liability Act ("Superfund")
- Safe Drinking Water Act
- Toxic Substances Control Act
- Federal Insecticide, Fungicide, and Rodenticide Act
- Surface Mining and Reclamation Act
- Community-Right-to-Know Law

Occupational Safety and Health Acts may also bear on environmental factors. Moreover, the Securities and Exchange Commission has demonstrated a compelling interest in environmental auditing, since it may affect the valuation of companies whose stocks are traded publicly.

Most environmental auditing carried out by companies in the United States to date reflects a defensive and reactive attitude. In

American auditing practice, "environmental" usually carries an unspoken modifier: "as defined by law." Thus, if Congress or other bodies have not yet included an environmental impact in the purview of a law, it is generally ignored (unless major financial risks are present). American "compliance auditing," as it is often called, is directed toward compliance with federal, state, and local regulations and toward avoidance of legal liability. Such auditing developed earliest and most professionally in large corporations, especially those in industries whose discharges and emissions came under scrutiny early on and were subjected to regulations. Most large waste-generating firms now have internal audit programs and/or make use of outside auditing services.

American corporations still tend to see auditing in a relatively legalistic and narrowly technical perspective—as a means of fending off fines and lawsuits, and as a means of preparing to deal with government regulations which may require the attention of high-level management and sometimes serious corporate investment. People working in the auditing field sometimes speak of aiming to improve management "comfort" through assurance that systems to monitor and control defined environmental impacts are in place and operating well.

As one American textbook lists them (Cahill 1987), typical U.S. corporate objectives for environmental auditing are as follows:

- Assurance of compliance
- Definition of liabilities
- Protection against liabilities for company officials
- Fact-finding in acquisitions and mergers
- Tracking and reporting of compliance costs
- Information transfer among operating units
- Accountability of management

Since the mid-1980s it has been the practice of the U.S. Environmental Protection Agency (EPA) to strongly encourage serious auditing efforts by corporations. These are taken by the Agency as being good-faith attempts to reduce environmental impacts, and evidently such efforts tend to secure relatively generous treatment by the Agency when infractions are discovered and consent decrees are being negotiated. A company's established auditing program also may make EPA oversight and inspections more efficient in a period when EPA budgets have been tight. In addition, it is believed by many in EPA that the "proactive" approach embodied in auditing programs makes environmental catastrophes less likely.

Some American environmental auditing is carried on with tight security, closely supervised by the corporate legal department; this is to guard against public disclosure of information which may embarrass the company or leave it open to lawsuits. In such situations, audit reports are tightly guarded and made available only to top executives; sometimes they are given only orally.

There are, however, many American companies that distribute audit reports fairly widely to management. There are also notable cases, such as public utilities, which must maintain open relationships with their public utility commissions and thus make their reports easily available.

In the United Kingdom most environmental audits, especially those done by large consulting groups, are commissioned by U.S. companies operating overseas. As in the United States, virtually all of this auditing is compliance auditing (Elkington 1990). The basic stance of these companies is still defensive. The shift of perception that occurred in a considerable portion of German management over the past decade has not yet happened in British companies.

Environmental Data Services Ltd. of London has reported on the environmental performance of companies for over ten years. Although these company profiles are not formal audits, they provide an excellent indication of how an external organization can monitor industry's environmental performance (Elkington 1987, 61).

Similar profiles, audits, and research data bases of corporate social and environmental performance have grown in the United States as a result of several factors. The growing $625 billion social investment movement has been one market for social and environmental analyses of corporations. Some investment funds, such as Working Assets Common Holdings or Calvert Social Investment Funds, maintain their own in-house research departments. Several private consulting firms and nonprofit research groups that investigate corporate social and environmental activity provide such information to the public for a modest charge.

Milton Moskowitz's book *The 100 Best Companies to Work for in America* (Moskowitz, Levering, and Katz 1993), updated regularly, addresses social and environmental issues, but places a special emphasis on conditions within the company that influence employee morale, loyalty, and performance. For example, although Levi Strauss is noted for a remarkable record on cultural diversity, charitable giving, community involvement, commitment to quality, environmental improvement, and employee participation, it was removed from Moskowitz's 1993 list for the precipitous closing (sixty days' notice to thousands of long-tenure Levi's employees) of its manufacturing plants in Texas to cut costs through socially and ecologically less sound offshore production.

The Council on Economic Priorities maintains a data base on corporate environmental practices as well as audit reports and research information used to prepare its annual *Shopping for a Better World.* The guide rates the social and environmental performance of the manufacturers of hundreds of popular consumer products. Any company rated in the U.S. guide is required to fill out its own internal audit report, which is then reviewed against external data. CEP's British affiliate, New Consumer, has its own ranking system designed for companies in the United Kingdom. The *Asahi Journal* in Japan published a special 1991 edition which surveyed seventy self-ranking Japanese companies on similar criteria, appropriate to Japan's corporate context. Its 1993 edition will include information from government and independent sources.

In the United States, the Coalition for Environmentally Responsible Economics (CERES) established the CERES Principles (1990), formerly called the Valdez Principles, in response to the Exxon oil spill (see Appendix B). The Principles are designed to serve as a baseline standard of ecological responsibility which companies will agree to comply with voluntarily, much as the Sullivan Principles became a standard that changed corporate practices in South Africa and supported efforts to eliminate apartheid. Signatories are required to conduct an annual audit and submit the results, which can be subject to external review. CERES is committed to including not only "clean" companies as signatories of the Principles but also companies that demonstrate consistent improvement.

Corporate momentum has yet to build in support of the CERES Principles. Many companies fear that going public with an environmental or social commitment places them under more stringent media scrutiny. Companies that vow to improve their ecological performance are held to a higher standard—and can draw more negative publicity for their weaknesses than companies whose track record is much worse but who don't try to change.

One of the most significant contributions of CERES, and other similar efforts, could be the establishment of standards for what will become generally accepted ecological principles, much like the generally accepted accounting principles that evolved over nearly a decade of dialogue and experimentation with scores of U.S. companies in the 1930s. Such standards can guide ecological reporting procedures that will be required and verified by outside auditors, as are corporate financial statements. Pioneer companies like Ben & Jerry's, Patagonia, and Esprit with its ecollection clothing line are investigating ways to develop ecological accounting systems, generating demand on the corporate side. The United Nations is also active in this area.

A system that numerically approximates both positive and negative ecological impacts gets attention. Such ecological accounting would offer a new bottom line by which to evaluate companies. This should prove a sounder criterion for evaluating the value and potential of companies in the future. Investors and shareholders may increasingly use ecological sustainability rather than narrow profitability as a criterion for evaluating corporate long-term strategic positioning. The environmental movement must join more aggressively with the growing cadre of ecological economists to tackle the complex job of developing standards and designing implementable accounting procedures to accurately report corporate ecological performance.

The International Chamber of Commerce (ICC) has taken a leading role in championing environmental auditing, but a quick glance at its 1988 pamphlet, *Environmental Auditing*, indicates that it limits itself to compliance auditing. Moreover, perhaps anticipating more stringent regulations and public scrutiny, the ICC paper insists that it is "essential that the procedure should be seen as the responsibility of the company itself, and should be voluntary and for company use only" (ICC 1988, 12).

Environmental audits are an essential step in minimizing the most serious and massive environmental impacts of modern industry. These American practices are already being adopted to some degree in Europe. We believe that all responsible governments should create or extend environmental regulations so that auditing of this type will be adopted as rapidly as possible in all corporations operating throughout the world. Regulations alone are unlikely to result, however, in new or creative thinking about large aspects of a company's operations. For this, innovative methodologies are needed.

ENVIRONMENTAL DATA ANALYSIS: QUANTITY AND QUALITY

All ecologically oriented management practices, and auditing in particular, require a reliable information system for maintaining ecologically relevant data, beginning with a record of the environmental impacts or costs generated by the company's operations. And here we encounter a problem central to all methods of ecological data analysis. Most ecological impacts cannot be quantified precisely, since they affect the quality of life—human and nonhuman—which is basically determined by value judgments, although measurements can be useful in assessing them.

Conventional economics, and the discipline of business administration in particular, has traditionally been presented as a value-free science, even though values are of paramount importance for all social sciences (Capra 1982, 190). Instead of dealing with values, business traditionally attempts to equate values with prices, which are measurable quantities and can be treated as "objective." However, the criteria for attaching price tags to values, which essentially amount to political choices, are not made explicit.

The focus on prices not values perpetuates the tension between quantity and quality, between economics and ecology, which haunts all methods of ecological data analysis (Pfriem 1986, 223). This is quite evident in the various techniques of environmental accounting that lie at the origin of ecological auditing, as defined below. In the accounting system developed by the Swiss economist Ruedi Müller-Wenk (1980) during the late 1970s, the various environmental impact factors—energy consumption, resource consumption, water contamination, and so on—are quantified and recorded. The different factors are then compared to each other with the help of "equivalence coefficients" based on ecological scarcities. Thus, different companies, or the environmental impacts of one company in different years, can be compared.

The key problem with this method is how to determine the equivalence coefficients which give the method a scientific-mathematical appearance but at the same time mask an underlying political decision (Pfriem 1986, 219ff.). Moreover, the focus on scarcity as the only criterion ignores other ecological impacts, such as species extinction, and tends to emphasize the ecological status quo rather than the need for restoration.

METHODS OF ENVIRONMENTAL AUDITING

The methodology of environmental auditing is well developed, and several textbooks summarize it thoroughly (see Appendix A).

Generally companies possess written permits for specified maximum discharge quantities, and auditors (who usually work in teams of several people and spend several days in a given plant) begin their work by assembling and verifying these permits. Since large companies keep records of discharges and other environmental effects of their operations, auditors check a sampling of these records against permitted levels. They also physically inspect plants and investigate recording and reporting procedures to determine if they are providing reliable information. In some cases auditors may carry out independent laboratory tests, for example, of emissions.

In inspecting plants, auditors are trained to observe closely many key facilities: fuel and chemical tanks and their surrounding catchments, stacks, discharge lines, recovery systems, storage facilities, alarm systems, transportation practices, and so on. Detailed protocols or checklists, adapted in advance of likely problems in a given plant, are employed to ensure complete coverage of possible trouble spots. Questionnaires and direct interviewing techniques are both used to gather information. Laboratory test procedures are checked. Operating manuals, records, reports to outside agencies, and other management documents are scrutinized; and attempts are made to determine whether manuals and procedures are followed by staff—which is often difficult.

Sometimes flow charts of a plant's processes are prepared, facilitating an evaluation of whether management control is adequate. Since employee safety regulations and environmental regulations have some degree of overlap (e.g., regarding hazardous substances used in production processes), auditors also concern themselves with safety, including worker safety gear and emergency plans. Noise, dust, and odors, which may affect both employees and neighbors of the plant, are also scrutinized.

As the audit proceeds, tentative report materials are transmitted to management for comment and discussion. These form the basis for the final report delivered at the end of the audit. This report provides an evaluation of company compliance with relevant regulations and also notes problem areas requiring attention.

METHODS OF ECOLOGICAL AUDITING

We review below a number of methods of ecological data collection and analysis. (These methods are more fully detailed in F. Senn's doctoral dissertation, "Ecological Business Management," cited in Steger 1988.) Some of these methods are used in general business practice in other contexts and have been around for a very long time; some date from the social auditing of the 1960s and 1970s; some have been adapted from environmental auditing; and some have been developed, particularly in Germany and Switzerland, during the late 1970s and 1980s. As we will explain in later chapters, ecological auditing is more comprehensive than compliance or environmental auditing, and its repertoire of methodologies is broader.

In Germany and Switzerland, auditing in many companies has gone well beyond government regulations to an examination of the "ecological compatibility" of a company's operations. The task is not only to verify compliance with fixed standards but also to minimize environmental impact. This includes protection of employees and the community, provision of an ecologically healthy workplace, and manufacture of "eco-friendly" goods. Such broader concerns are only beginning to appear in the thinking of American environmental auditors, even though they are often dealt with by corporations in other perspectives.

Successful use of eco-auditing procedures will depend on the extent to which they enable an auditor to overcome the tension between economics and ecology by integrating qualitative and quantitative approaches.

Environmental Indicators. Environmental indicators such as "biological oxygen demand" (BOD) identify specific pollutants defined by governmental regulations. While providing a quantitative standard, the indicator method tends to ignore synergistic effects and involves value judgments that are not made explicit.

Environmental Accounting. Types of inputs and outputs (e.g., raw materials use, effluents, waste heat) are selected and quantified to show that the "true cost," which includes environmental impacts, clearly exceeds market price. Therefore, even expensive alternatives which are *less* ecologically damaging can be economically justified for the economy as a whole. Analysis, comparison, and evaluation of inputs and outputs are made possible through use of "equivalence coefficients"—a method which, though flawed, introduces ecological ethics into traditional economic analysis.

Environmental Impact Assessment. Originally based on the U.S. National Environmental Policy Act (1969), impact assessment represents an institutional check for compliance with environmental regulations. Environmental Impact Studies and Environmental Impact Reports use both quantitative measures (such as increases of traffic and air pollution) and qualitative ones (such as impacts on habitats of rare or endangered species). Similar procedures have been adopted by other nations, including Germany.

Economic Feasibility Calculations. This approach exclusively uses economic criteria with methods derived from accounting (for example, amortization and capital depreciation). However, these do not calculate whether investments or production processes are ecologically important or successful and cannot dissipate the tension between economics and ecology.

Technology Assessments. Like the environmental impact assessment, this method was developed for decision-making processes within governmental agencies. This deals specifically with the predicted social and political consequences of new technologies, but can integrate ecological considerations as well.

Material and Energy Auditing. This method, often incorporated in practical applications, can be especially useful in analyzing environmentally harmful "microprocesses" in a business, but can also serve as a permanent material flow matrix. A special feature of these physical measurements is that they can be used as criteria for establishing acceptable pollutant limits for environmental protection.

Market or Survey Research. This means gathering information, through questionnaires and controlled experiments, about the demand for ecologically friendly products, how much consumers are willing to pay for them, and the degree of public environmental consciousness either generally or on specific issues.

Cost-Benefit Analysis. This method evaluates outcomes to investors and others (such as employees) directly affected by an activity. Although it attempts to provide precise calculations of all effects, problems remain in establishing a monetary equivalent for different perceived outcomes.

Social Balance Sheet. The traditional concept of the "balance sheet" describing an enterprise in terms of financial assets and liabilities is extended to include relevant ecological and social costs as well as benefits.

Environmental Data Banks. Data banks are actually sources of information rather than instruments of analysis, but their inclusion here is justified by the increased importance of information retrieval within the audit planning procedure. So far, several data banks are used in Germany to facilitate and improve ecological planning processes. Data banks provide information on environmental conditions, ecological standards, pollutant threshold values, and literature references. The following data banks are widely used:

- UMPLIS (general information and document system)

- AWIDAT (waste management information)

- DABAWAS (water pollutant data)

Checklists. Checklists have evolved as a fundamental tool of both eco-auditing and narrower compliance auditing. Often checklists have been compiled on an ad hoc basis and lack logical rigor. The central task lies in compiling a systematic listing of the complex ecological relationships involved in production and consumption. These conceptual aids can then stimulate decision making via categorizing and comparing factors. (See Chapters 7–10 for our summary of checklists.)

Decision Tree Method. Useful for decision-making methods where conflicting ecological aims exist, this method involves ordering goals into a hierarchy and then ranking subgoals with respect to their contribution toward achieving higher goals.

System Dynamics. Complex simulation of system processes is here made possible through computer analysis. This costly method was developed by J. Forrester to simulate economic and ecological growth processes, and has been applied to certain global models.

Scenario Building. This technique is useful for developing broad participation in a company's ecological planning. In the "Future Lab" version of the techniques developed in Germany by Robert Jungk and Rüdiger Lutz (Lutz 1981), discussion groups are asked to develop alternative possible scenarios for the future:

- The status quo scenario

- A positive alternate scenario

- A realistic counter scenario

- A strategic scenario as a synthesis of the first three

While techniques such as cost-benefit analyses require expert preparation and focus on specialized problems, scenarios are opportunities to interrelate many factors in the company as they are perceived or envisioned by a broad sample of people. Thus, they are useful for seeing the relationships between individual or departmental concerns and the future of the company as a whole. Since they set up alternative basic paradigms, they also tend to stimulate creative and innovative thinking.

It is to be hoped that a proactive, creative approach to broad and comprehensive auditing ("ecological auditing," as we shall define it in subsequent chapters of this report) will develop boldly throughout the world. In view of the strong encouragement of the U.S. Environmental Protection Agency, the continuing concern with energy efficiency, the growing demand for "eco-friendly" products, and the worldwide influence of European product eco-labeling standards, a shift in perception similar to the one that emerged in the German corporate community during the 1980s is likely to get underway soon in the American corporate community.

Indeed, there are already entrepreneurs in the United States and Britain who have adopted an ecologically conscious management style in their companies and are now experimenting with creative approaches to ecological auditing. In the following chapter, we present profiles of some of these companies, both in Europe and the United States.

3

INNOVATIVE ECOMANAGEMENT PRACTICES AND PROGRAMS WORLDWIDE

It is easy to tell people how to be environmentally friendly. It is easy to promise what you intend to do in the future. But in my mind the number of green people declines when we talk about true round-the-clock environmentalists, those who live like they teach; we cut out the talkers and look at what people have achieved instead of what they intend to do.

—RUGER FRIBERG, VOLVO

To many companies and industries, making business ecologically sustainable sounds like "pie in the sky." To environmentalists, the challenges of preserving jobs and economic viability while executing massive corporate change may seem trivial. This chapter highlights notable innovations instituted by both "pioneer" and "mainstream" companies, practices consistent with ecomanagement or systemic management principles. (Profiles of some of the companies used as examples can be found in Steger 1988.)

GOOD PRACTICES

Small, privately held companies can be remarkably agile in changing company practices. Smith & Hawken, a California mail-order company selling gardening supplies, housewares, and clothing, is one of the businesses that has conducted a wide-ranging eco-audit along the lines we suggest. Concern for the environment has always been an important part of the company's philosophy, but in December 1989 Smith & Hawken began a more formal (even though not initially systematic) audit. Several months later, one result of the audit was an environmental policy statement for 1990, made available to all customers ("Environmental Action" 1990).

The actions initiated by the audit include widespread recycling and reuse of materials, a companywide ban on styrofoam, elimination of toxics and plastic wherever possible, numerous energy- and water-saving measures, and support for bicycling as a means of transportation to and from work. In addition, Smith & Hawken conducted in-depth studies on the history and forest management of teak to ensure that their teak furniture (from Javanese tree farms) is environmentally sound. They also donated money to rain forest groups and offered their business as a testing ground for developing teak certification programs.

One of Smith & Hawken's most remarkable actions as part of their eco-audit has been to question the ecological sustainability of the industry to which the company belongs: the mail-order business. (We suggest such evaluations as this in Chapter 4.) In a four-page statement, "The Junk Stops Here," cofounder Paul Hawken reviewed the excessive and wasteful practices of the catalog and direct-mail industry (including many environmental organizations!), and set forth a number of guidelines adopted by the company to counteract the disastrous environmental impact of this trend. These include the following:

- Catalogs printed on recycled and recyclable paper
- A "sanctuary forest program" in which two or three trees are planted on degraded habitat for each tree used by the company
- Use of soy-based inks

- Publication of the catalog in separate subsections tailored to customers' needs in order to avoid sending unwanted coverage to each customer
- A more responsible policy regarding the rental of mailing lists
- No changes in the catalog for extended periods to avoid seasonal "remailing"
- A special service to help customers reduce their junk mail

Minnesota Mining and Manufacturing (3M) boasts one of the oldest waste prevention programs in the United States. Founded on the premise that environmental protection and financial strength were linked, 3M's 3P (Pollution Prevention Pays) Program has saved over $500 million through over 2500 process changes and an additional $650 million through energy conservation (Leighton 1992). They do not profit from air emission credits earned through their efforts, but rather return them to environmental agencies for air quality improvement efforts. 3M has consistently raised its environmental goals while integrating ecology into companywide strategy and operations. They have found ways to implement closed-loop systems in which waste is reused as product, like production line scrap that is now used to make minibooms, and industrial pillows used to contain and absorb oil spills at sea (Smart 1992).

Hanna Andersson, a children's clothing company, gives customers credit on future purchases for returning outgrown Hanna clothing. Tens of thousands of "Hannadowns" have been donated to abused women and children. From a marketing perspective, the program proves the product's durability while helping the needy and boosting sales and customer/employee loyalty alike.

Around the mid-1980s, numerous European companies began to adopt simple ecological practices like recycling programs, energy-saving measures, reusable containers, and so forth. Some of them went much further and began to move toward a more comprehensive ecologically oriented management. A German chemical company (SKW Trostberg), for example, not only redesigned its production processes to make them less ecologically damaging, but also instituted employee information and motivation programs, and gave financial support to environmental organizations and various environmental impact studies. A leading mail-order business (Otto Versand) audited its product offerings and eliminated particularly harmful products from its stock, including items made of rain-forest wood or involving the killing of endangered species. (Otto Versand was profiled in *Der Spiegel,* no. 16, April 1989.)

A cosmetic company in Hamburg (Elida Gibbs) strives for exemplary openness in its "Green Reports," maintains contacts with leading environmental activists, and created a companywide "eco-team" consisting of representatives of all departments. A manufacturer of industrial supplies (Friedrich Niemann) publishes a "Green Catalogue" of eco-technologies.

A Swiss supermarket (Coop Schweiz) developed its own eco-labeling system. A beer brewery (Neumarkter Lammsbräu) pioneered a "holistic management philosophy" that includes organic agriculture, ecologically sound brewing and packaging processes, and utilization of solar energy.

Most of these exemplary companies conduct partial ecological audits, and a few even developed comprehensive auditing systems. One of those is Winter & Sons, an industrial company in Hamburg producing diamond cutting tools, which developed the Winter model discussed above. Another trendsetter has been Bischof & Klein, one of Europe's largest packaging companies, which designed a comprehensive "eco-blueprint" as a guideline for its corporate policies (see Steger 1988, 263). Moreover, it was the first industrial enterprise in Germany to initiate a systematic ecological audit involving three levels: a company audit, product audits, and process audits. This system has been so successful that Bischof & Klein now plan to offer it to other companies.

In England, The Body Shop, a cosmetic company founded by Anita and Gordon Roddick, is engaged in ecological practices of similar depth and pioneering quality ("Environmental Management" 1990). The company's culture and activities are based on its founders' vision of a successful business activity promoting environmental and social issues and working these into its day-to-day practices. Since the opening of its first outlet in 1976, The Body Shop has grown into an international network of over 450 shops

in thirty-seven countries, founded on a number of common ecological principles:

- To sell cosmetics with minimal hype and packaging
- To promote health rather than glamour
- To use natural ingredients wherever possible
- Not to test ingredients or final products on animals
- To provide a refill service in all shops
- To recycle waste and use recycled paper wherever possible

The company buys raw materials from all over the world and
has a policy of sustainable, nonexploitative trade agreements with
communities in economically disadvantaged countries. A key characteristic of The Body Shop is to use its show windows, carrier bags,
and other select items for radical, highly unconventional campaigns
about a wide range of environmental and human-rights issues.

From its beginning, The Body Shop has had a clear top-level
commitment to ensuring environmental and social excellence. Environmental concerns are incorporated into every aspect of its operations. Due to the recent expansion of the business, the need for a
formal approach to ecologically conscious management was recognized. The company decided to have an all-embracing audit with
the goal of producing a formal environmental policy statement.

Many of the techniques recommended in this book are prac-
ticed by The Body Shop. They include effective multimedia communication, both internally and externally; supportive relationships
with grass-roots organizations; staff training programs with strong
environmental emphasis; ecological purchasing standards and product development; and an extensive waste management program. So
far, The Body Shop's audit has covered only the offices and ware-
houses at the company's headquarters. An expansion to include the
shops and subsidiary companies was not undertaken at this first stage,
because it was felt that the methodology of such all-embracing audits
is still poorly developed. However, further steps are planned for the
future.

Volvo, based in Sweden, is linking environment with its hall-
marks of safety and quality as core elements of corporate strategy.

Volvo has developed new internal accounting for environmental technology investments because while it may be costly, top management is confident it should improve sales and customer loyalty. Volvo is working with suppliers to co-manage redesigning the taxonomy of its parts and materials to facilitate disassembly, recycled materials use, and the elimination of ecologically unsound materials. Life-cycle analysis at Volvo is broken into raw materials use, production, end-use (car ownership), and recycling/disposal. They are investigating on-board navigation computers to reduce wrong turns, clogged streets, and parking headaches, as well as hybrid electric/combustion cars and new, light, strong, recyclable materials design. Future plans include collaborative goal-setting with supplier industries, government, and other auto companies.

BMW of North America is investigating the feasibility of establishing a network of authorized BMW recycling centers in the United States to support BMW's engineering design toward recycling. The Big Three—General Motors, Ford, and Chrysler—are exploring a vehicle recycling partnership. The creation of new business serving those needs is being linked through the Automotive Dismantlers and Recyclers Association, now boasting over 2,200 members internationally (*Business and the Environment* 1992, 4).

Bad Brückenauer Mineralbrunnen, a German mineral-water company, carried out a complete eco-audit of its entire facilities, developing its own measurements and instruments because there were no precedents in their industry. Now other cities and water-producing communities (such as Bad Pyrmont) have adapted their innovative approach.

Royal Dutch/Shell is one of the pioneers in adapting the scenario technique for business planning. Every two to three years, Shell updates its global scenarios. These scenarios, or "stories," are then the basis for internal business decisions.

Every industry and company should explicate two to three scenarios to explore the larger context of development. Such scenarios help plans for ecological transformation become practical. Shell, for example, derived a "sustainable world" scenario (see Figure 2 below) by simply extrapolating its own future into the larger context of world economy and ecology, and came to the surprising conclusion that, despite the enormous challenges, it should change from the oil business to ecologically sustainable enterprise. Time will tell if and when that awareness translates into transformed business practice at Shell. Major change by an industrial giant in a strategic industry like oil could have a dramatic impact on the earth, on health, on daily life, and on the speed of other businesses' actions toward sustainability.

Fig. 2.   A Sample Corporate Scenario

	Global Mercantilism	Sustainable World
Challenge	Hegemonic decline and economic instability	Degradation of the environment (especially through global warming)
Response	Multipolar world and mercantilism	International cooperation and management
Implications For Energy	New rules for business and reconfiguration of markets	New values for fuels and reconstruction of the energy industry

Source: A. Kahane, *Global Scenarios for the Energy Industry: Challenge and Response,* Shell International Petroleum Company, Ltd., England, 1991, p.9

Promostyle and Trend Union are two "trend services" in the fashion industry that consider environmental concerns of pivotal importance. A recent Promostyle book aimed at the trade was dedicated to "Ecostyle" and argued that environmentalism is going to dramatically change our aesthetic. Promostyle's conferences in New York, Tokyo, and Paris brought together trade associations, manufacturers, and retailers. Panelists from companies like Patagonia, Nike, and Esprit discussed ecological company culture, the need for ecological clothing to maintain market share, design and production innovations, and changing the relationships between earth and the retailer, the customer and the retailer, manufacturers and designers.

Nike is using postindustrial recycled rubber in the soles of shoes (a practice being used in several industries, including computers and automobiles). Nike is also looking at the end-life of the shoe. Each part (upper, mid-sole cushion, and sole) would be able to be separated so that it could be recycled. By using the same synthetic materials in different forms (foam, tread, fabric), a whole shoe could be easily recyclable. Full life-cycle analysis to find substitutes for toxic synthetics is a further step.

Levi's routinely recycles clothing scrap for labels and has joined Esprit, O-Wear, Seventh Generation, and Patagonia in mass producing clothing from organically grown cotton.

Esprit's ecollection goes several steps further. This line of clothing has consistently been at the forefront of new innovations, a genuine marriage of social, environmental, and sustainable concerns. The line uses organic cotton, knits, tencel, and wool. The clothing is adorned with tagua nut buttons bought from indigenous people's co-ops in the rain forest, and wooden hand-painted buttons from Appalachian women's co-ops. The ecollection adheres to strict human rights, labor protection, and environmental standards in production. The designs are classic rather than trendy to discourage consumerism. Natural and low-impact dyes are used, as well as organic cotton that actually grows in colors. Esprit International, based in Germany, is mainstreaming these innovations into selected regular clothing lines through the Blue Planet program.

Esprit's Ecodesk is responsible for a vast array of programs, from charitable giving to paid lunches at the in-house organic cafeteria and an on-premises health club complete with yoga and aerobics classes. Employees are reimbursed for several hours of volunteer work at local nonprofit organizations. They receive one day of vacation time for every thirty days they come to work using mass transportation or bicycle. Esprit will split the price of tickets to cultural events. A lecture series brings in famous environmentalists, feminists, and social activists; and company courses on social and environmental issues are available to staff.

"Cradle-to-grave" strategies that consider the entire production cycle, from raw materials to responsible waste disposal, are being replaced by "cradle-to-cradle" solutions that transform waste into new product. 3M's CCBA (Coordinate Chemical Bonding Adsorption) process treats hazardous and nonhazardous industrial sludge, turning it into aggregate pellets used in concrete, insulation, and roofing tiles. The process creates no air pollution or waste by-products. Designing products from waste generated from the company's current operations can "close the loop" of waste emissions. In addition to the positive ecological impact, cutting waste treatment and disposal costs can combine with new product sales for greater company profitability.

Several chemical companies, notorious for environmental and health violations, have shifted from seeing themselves as low-price commodity producers to industrial marketers, driven by customer needs. The result has often been a linking of environmental improvement with marketability in the effort to enhance customer service. Union Carbide has worked with paint customers to make solvent-free paint. S. C. Johnson's switch to nontoxic substances for its Raid insecticide created a value-added specialty business out of a price-based commodity business (Butcher and Feld 1992).

Despite stronger corporate environmental improvements at United Technologies dating from the late 1970s, Environmental Protection Agency regulators saw little consistency between plant locations and no process to ensure continual compliance mandated by a serious commitment at the top. In the eighties, the company took a major step toward ecological transformation beyond the regulations contained in the 35,000 pages of federal environmental laws. United Technologies' CEO, Robert F. Daniell, emphasized environmental issues in five primary areas: training, assessment and auditing, environmental electronic data base development, waste minimization, and legislative and regulatory proactivity.

In addition to strengthening the role of corporate environmental staff in relation to operating units, environmental standards were raised within United Technologies and a new corporate policy on human and natural resource protection was developed and disseminated. Environmental issues began to be treated as core business issues. This was marked by the establishment in 1990 of a senior vice president position, responsible for environmental and business practices, with direct access to the CEO, and the establishment of similar executive positions at each operating unit with direct access to both the environmental senior vice president and their own business unit presidents. The structure was inspired by surveying the practices of peer companies with strong environmental leadership records.

Several companies are setting stricter standards on suppliers with whom they do business. Levi Strauss & Co. and Reebok are among the companies that refuse to do business with manufacturers who employ child labor, prison or forced labor, maintain unsafe and unhealthy work conditions, use corporal punishment, or operate in nations with pervasive human-rights violations. Esprit's ecollection and Ecodesk take a more proactive stance, requiring strong ecological performance and a willingness to reduce packaging and use recycled materials. ecollection, for example, is encouraging its cooperative supplier in Ghana to plant trees to replace the wood used in firing glass buttons before Esprit will increase its orders. Apple Computer and Hewlett-Packard are among the computer companies that have made it easy for customers to recycle laser printer toner cartridges at no charge.

Xerox Corporation began linking environmental improvement efforts to health and safety issues in 1980, but the 1984 Bhopal disaster motivated Xerox to link environmental improvement to total quality. Preventive measures proved costly—over $50 million in proactive environmental remediation greatly exceeded the cost of mere compliance—yet commitment from senior management reduced future liabilities and reduced operating costs in many cases. Management commitment was maintained despite stiff competition from IBM, Kodak, and the Japanese.

For example, chlorine storage problems were identified by Xerox. After reducing chlorine stored at a site near a nursing home, chlorine was moved to an altogether different site until it was eliminated from the manufacturing process. Locations worldwide that used industrial solvents were surveyed to identify possible ground-water or soil contamination. Where deposits were found, government agencies were notified and worked with to develop and implement this voluntary remedial action. Disposal of dangerous selenium and arsenic alloy-coated photoreceptor drums was eliminated by recycling and remanufacturing new drums from the old at a fraction of the cost. Xerox reclaims about one million finished piece parts worldwide and saves nearly $200 million.

Xerox is researching "cradle-to-cradle" technologies, ways that waste products can be used as raw materials for other products. Waste toner is being developed for plastic pigmentation, asphalt additives, plastic lumber, and gaskets. CFC elimination has been a major pledge. Biodegradable cleaners have been substituted for toxic chemical solvents by over 90 percent in most facilities. In addition to positive environmental impact, $400,000 in hazardous waste disposal expenses have been avoided. Moreover, the company has made a commitment to continuous improvement once current benchmarks are reached.

Xerox's employee involvement component of its quality improvement efforts has resulted in a commitment to customer concern for the environment. Awareness of imminent global environmental legislation was another motivator. Postconsumer recycled waste makes up Xerox packaging now, saving about $2 million per year. There has been dramatic packaging reduction as well.

"Doing the right thing" is now seen as the best path to long-term profitability, according to Paul Allaire, Xerox CEO. Senior managers comprise the Environmental Leadership Steering Committee, which directs environmental programs and reports quarterly on results. Committed individuals companywide are encouraged to take initiative and can join an internal company environmental network.

Consumer pressure to strengthen corporate ecological practices can take a major international form. Among the largest offshore customers of U.S. agribusiness are Japanese food-buying cooperatives. One key purchasing criterion is food purity. Their growing concern about pesticide use may push key agribusiness suppliers toward more organic farming practices (Leighton 1992).

AGENTS OF CHANGE

The International Network for Environmental Management (INEM)

Starting in 1985, a number of innovative companies got together in several countries to form environmental management associations. Several of these associations in turn established the International Network for Environmental Management (INEM) on February 19, 1991. The goal of INEM's international activities is that as many companies as possible should practice environmental management as soon as possible. In order to achieve this goal, INEM has worked out recommendations for industry, government, and administrative departments in various countries.

In the framework of the United Nations Conference on Environment and Development (UNCED), INEM organized the International Industry Conference for Sustainable Development from June 2 to 5, 1992, with participation of INEM national member organizations and many of the member companies in these organizations. In total, INEM member organizations represent more than 600 companies, and affiliated associations more than 400 companies.

A number of INEM members (the associations in Germany and South Africa) and an affiliate (Switzerland) have developed Codes of Practice for environmental matters. INEM also supports the "Business Charter for Sustainable Development—Principles for Environmental Management" adopted by the International Chamber of Commerce in April 1991 and the "Global Environmental Charter" of the Confederation of Japanese Industry (*Keidanren*). These are important steps, but there is still a long way to go in this work. It is highly desirable that the international business community give more support to INEM and systematically use the opportunities it offers for cooperative action.

National Business Associations for Environmental Management

Following the establishment of B.A.U.M. (German Environmental Management Association) in 1985, the integrated system of environmental management became increasingly well known in

Germany. The main reason for this was that the media were reporting in detail on concrete pilot projects for environmental management in industry. Interest grew quickly in the other German-speaking countries, Austria and Switzerland.

In the European Year of the Environment (1987/1988), the Commission of the European Communities took up the issue of environmental management. This was done through actions such as the establishment of the European Better Environment Awards for industry, and through publication of the book *Business and the Environment* (Winter et al. 1989) in several languages. The subject was dealt with increasingly at international conferences. Beginning in 1989, several national organizations for environmental management were started each year. From that time onward, it is reasonable to talk about an international movement for environmental management.

This movement was significantly influenced by the report of the World Commission on Environment and Development (the "Brundtland Report"), which appeared in 1987 and presented the concept of "sustainable development" to the public. The basic idea of the concept is to meet the needs of present generations without jeopardizing the capability of future generations to meet their needs.

National business associations for environmental management were set up in Austria, Switzerland, South Africa, Sweden, the United Kingdom, Denmark, Brazil, and Israel in close collaboration with B.A.U.M. Germany and INEM. Comparable organizations, independent of B.A.U.M., were formed in the United States, Japan, and Hong Kong. Cooperation between the national environmental management associations is becoming more intensive and more comprehensive year by year.

Several national associations of companies for environmental management for Austria, Brazil, Denmark, Germany, South Africa, Sweden, and the United Kingdom have been linked to the International Network for Environmental Management (INEM) since 1991. (Additional national associations are currently intensifying their collaboration with INEM and its member associations.)

Trade associations in industries that have been targeted for repeated or particularly severe environmental regulation violations have quickly established their own environmental guidelines and environmental sections of the association. Several of these efforts in petroleum, chemical, drug, and military manufacturing have developed intensive public relations campaigns to demonstrate their environmental concerns concurrent with continued litigation for polluting. For example, Stephan Schmidheiny, a key figure in the formation of the Business Roundtable on Sustainable Development, had one of his major holdings cited for repeated violation of pollution standards. The company's response was to aggressively litigate rather than clean up. Ironically, this came to light merely months after the UNCED Earth Summit in Rio and release of the Roundtable's book *Changing Course* (Schmidheiny 1992).

The following sections present some of the important national associations for environmental management. It should also be noted that scores of regional and local groups are constantly being established within the United States and other large countries throughout the world.

Associations in the United States

Industry and professional associations are addressing ecological concerns, in many cases through a separate environmental section. The most notable trade group to watch may be in the industrial design field. Industrial designers stand at the forefront of determining the nature of products and materials, habits and tastes for decades to come. The profession's environmental wing has been addressing sustainable design in conferences and exploring cutting-edge solutions to ecological design challenges.

Other organizations provide networking support for companies seeking to make genuine improvements. The Social Investment Forum (SIF), founded in 1984, is a national professional association of socially and environmentally responsible financial advisors. SIF founders include the founder of CERES, socially and environmentally screened mutual funds, pension funds, venture capital firms, banks, investors, and community loan funds that lend to housing developments and businesses adhering to social and environmental criteria and controlled by the predominantly low-income people served.

The Social Venture Network (SVN), founded in 1987, is a membership organization composed primarily of entrepreneurs, investors, and investment professionals. Members see business not only as a means to financial success but also as a potentially powerful force in creating a world that is more

- Just—in which the gap between extremely rich and poor people is reduced and prejudice of all kinds is eradicated
- Humane—in which land, food, education, and shelter are available to all and where torture and other forms of violence are eliminated
- Sustainable—in which human patterns, including how goods and services are produced and consumed, are altered to assure the survival of the planet

SVN addresses questions of business management and social impact by focusing on

- Creating a better **product** such as improved quality of housing, pollution-free manufacturing, prevention-centered health care, nutritious food products, and ecologically sound land development.
- Developing a better **process** to manage business through employee participation in management or ownership, creation of a more caring and satisfying work environment for employees, and production methods that conserve and replenish limited natural resources
- Exploring innovative uses of **profit** including profit sharing and corporate and personal philanthropy that befits the entrepreneurial spirit
- Addressing **community issues** out of an understanding that business affects community health and can help foster more vibrant cities and neighborhoods

In addition to providing public interest leadership consistent with SVN's purpose, members must have been involved in creating a company or nonprofit organization with over $5 million in revenues or must be an officer of a company with revenue or assets in excess of $250 million. Occasional exceptions are made for visionary, entrepreneurial leaders from the nonprofit world whose innovative thinking and practices have had a strong influence on business.

Businesses for Social Responsibility (BSR) was established as the voice for progressive business leaders in the United States, a counterweight to the U.S. Chamber of Commerce. Founded in 1992 with fifty-five companies nationwide, members include Reebok, Lotus, Aveda, Esprit, Calvert Group, and Rhino Records. BSR members adhere to the following:

- Advocate integrating long-term social and environmental considerations with the need for profit in business planning and decision making in public policy

- Strive to manage their businesses in ways that will safeguard the health and safety of their employees and enrich the communities in which they do business

- Make a commitment to manufacturing and distributing high-quality products and services that are safe and are ethically packaged, marketed, and sold

- Promote equal opportunity in the ways they hire and relate to their employees and by encouraging the development of sound, long-term business opportunities accessible to all

- Press for public policies of concern to business that foster sustainable development and global security

Businesses for Social Responsibility builds public awareness, provides networking and educational support to the business community, and lobbies nationally and locally on the full range of issues concerning business: marketplace, workplace, local community, domestic policy, and international policy. Business Partnerships for Peace, a similarly focused organization with overlapping membership, became part of BSR in January 1993.

The Global Environmental Management Initiative (GEMI) was founded in March 1990 by major corporations, with the goal of persuading business worldwide to adopt policies of Environmental Excellence. It aims to promote worldwide business ethics based on environmental management and sustainable development. GEMI also wishes to promote the efforts of the business world in environmental solutions and leadership, and advance the dialogue between the business world and the interested public. GEMI has five main goals:

- To promote critical thinking and the exchange of ideas in environmental management

- To raise the environmental performance level of companies throughout the world by giving practical examples and demonstrating environmental management and sustainable development

- To achieve unity with forces in society for a global code of business ethics that is oriented toward environmental management and sustainable development

- To promote dialogue between business circles and the interested public

- To create partnerships throughout the world and to promote similar endeavors in other countries

GEMI sponsored a convention in January 1991 in Washington, D.C., on the subject of "Corporate Quality/Environmental Management," and a further convention in March 1992. The purpose was to encourage application of the principles of Total Quality Management (TQM) to environmental management. The Total Quality Management project was also the subject of a seminar held by GEMI at the World Industry Conference on Environmental Management in Rotterdam on April 9, 1991.

The members of GEMI include Allied Signal, AT&T, Boeing, Digital Equipment Corporation, Dow Chemical, Eastman Kodak, Du Pont, ICI America, Occidental Petroleum, Philip Morris, Procter & Gamble, Union Carbide, and USX.

Several awards programs have been established that honor companies for social and/or ecological performance. As the Malcolm Baldridge Award recognizes top performers in Total Quality Management, the Council on Economic Priorities (described above) sponsors the Corporate Conscience Award. The Business Enterprise

Trust's Business Enterprise Awards honor companies that combine strong economic performance and creative moral purpose.

The National Wildlife Federation (NWF) established the Corporate Conservation Council in 1982 to provide a forum where up to twenty corporate executives representing diverse industries engage in frank and open discussions with NWF about emerging environmental and natural resource issues that can affect corporate policy. Members include Asea Brown Boveri, AT&T, Browning-Ferris, Ciba-Geigy, Duke Power, 3M, Procter & Gamble, Johnson & Johnson, and Waste Management. The Council has released policy statements on several environmental issues and developed a curriculum to introduce environmental issues into graduate schools of business administration. Their most recent gathering addressed sustainability (see Figure 3 below).

Fig. 3.   Working Principles for Sustainable Behavior

FOR ECOLOGICAL SECURITY

Protecting ecological systems to minimize their degradation
Preserving ecological systems to maintain critical services
Restoring ecological systems to enhance their productivity

FOR RESOURCE SECURITY

Economizing resources to obtain more with less
Conserving resources to extend and reallocate options
Substituting resource use for lower impact and renewable supply

FOR SOCIOECONOMIC SECURITY

Dispersing economic activity to broaden opportunity and benefit
Humanizing economic activity to promote fuller participation
Vitalizing economic activity to better fulfill basic needs

Corporate Conservation Council
National Wildlife Federation
Synergy 92 Conference
Laguna Niguel, California

There are several other examples of environmentalist/corporate dialogue that has led to changes in corporate practices. Earth Island Institute was pivotal to Safeway becoming the first U.S. supermarket chain to adopt policies against purchasing tuna caught by methods that kill dolphins. Fuji Photo consulted with the Audubon Society about its conversion from plastic to cardboard film canisters.

Small, private gatherings of CEOs can often explore more radical ecological transformation. These gatherings include mainstream companies and progressive companies alike. They are reserved for corporate leaders with the capacity to look reality squarely in the face, to not believe their own green propaganda, and to stay out of denial about the enormity of the problem and their company's responsibility for the problem. The starting point will be personally shared by corporate officers in matter-of-fact candor, like a Volvo executive's comment that "Our products create pollution, noise, and waste." Kris McDivitt, CEO of Patagonia, a company noted as a pioneer for its innovative social and ecological practices claimed, "I'm embarrassed when people talk about how much we're doing. It's nothing compared to what is needed. Patagonia is prepared to be a petri dish for whatever it will take to turn this company around ecologically. No one knows yet what sustainability really is."

Associations in Canada

The Canadian government has sponsored provincial advisory boards made up of representatives from industry, government, and environmental groups to guide government environmental policy. Canada's Business Council on National Issues (BCNI), a coalition of Canada's largest companies, has an Environmental Task Force that profiles leading-edge companies and puts forth environmental recommendations to BCNI members.

Loblaws, Canada's largest supermarket chain, is one company that has worked with environmentalists to reevaluate corporate practices. They invited Pollution Probe, a Toronto-based environmental group, to conduct an environmental analysis. They identified green products that Loblaws could develop and sell. Criteria included reducing raw materials used in manufacturing, eliminating toxic components, and using recycled materials in products and packaging (Carson and Moulden 1991).

Associations in Europe

Germany

B.A.U.M., the German Environmental Management Association (*Bundesdeutscher Arbeitskreis fur umweltbewusstes Management e.V.*) was founded in 1985 and currently has 380 members. It is the oldest and largest organization of its kind.

B.A.U.M. sponsors include medium-sized and large companies from manufacturing, trade, and service industries, together with business associations, chambers of commerce, public authorities, and private individuals. With a membership drawn from virtually all sectors of the economy, it operates with an honorary board of management and a full-time professional staff.

The goals of B.A.U.M. are to enhance the environmental responsibility of business, to spread know-how on how to reconcile environmental concerns with business success, and to introduce environmental management in as many companies as possible.

Austria

A group of Austrian businessmen got together in spring 1989 to set up an organization under the title *"Bundesweiter Arbeitskreis fur Umweltbewusstes Management."* Since then, B.A.U.M. Austria has held seminars and conferences on subjects such as "Ecological Budgeting," "The Green Office," "Holistic Environmental Management," and "Environmental Protection in the New Europe."

Switzerland

The Swiss Environmental Management Association (*Schweizerische Vereinigung fur Ökologisch Bewußte Unternehmensführung/Association Suisse pour l'Integration de l'Ecologie dans la Gestion des Entreprises*) was founded on March 15, 1989, and has more than 160 members, including Migros, Ciba-Geigy, Nestle, Swiss Bank Corporation, Anova Holding, Lever, and Holzstoff.

The *oikos* student initiative of St. Gallen University held a conference on "Opportunities in Environmental Management" on June 30, 1988. It was attended by about sixty business managers and prepared the ground for the foundation of the Swiss Environmental Management Association. The goal of the Swiss Environmental Management Association is to disseminate the ideas of environmental management in Switzerland, in particular by establishing environmental thinking at the senior management level. This purpose is achieved by the transmission of knowledge about ecology, the exchange of experience between member companies, the promotion of environmentally oriented education and research, and in particular by the formation of "action groups" focusing on specific subjects.

Sweden

The Swedish BAUM organization is called *Svenska BAUM Naringslivets Miljöforum.* It was established by Swedish businessmen on October 22, 1990. The objective is to encourage more environmental management in the Swedish economy, and to provide a forum for the exchange of opinions, experience, and know-how in this context.

Svenska BAUM has some forty-five member companies, including ABB Flakt, ASSI, Nobel Industrier, Electrolux, Ericsson, ICA Foretagen, IKEA, KABI, Modo, Swedish National Railways, Stena Line, Svenska Massan, Southern Power, Tetra Pak, and Volvo. All member organizations practice staff ecology training, or have plans for doing so. The majority use the techniques of eco-auditing.

United Kingdom

A number of companies, forming a cross section of British industry, met in November 1990 to set up TREE UK—Technology, Research and Enterprise for the Environment. The oldest among

Fig. 4. Environmental Awareness in the European Community

Environment more important	Survey result (%)	Economy more important
35	Belgium	8
40	Ireland	23
45	Netherlands	9
47	Spain	12
47	Greece	12
48	GB	11
50	EC average	9
50	W.Germany	3
55	Italy	6
55	Denmark	3
56	France	11
65	Luxembourg	6

Balance: equally important/don´t know

INEM The International Network for Environmental Management

Grafik: © imu – bildinfo, Essen

Which would you favor if faced with conflicting interests: environment or industry? On average, every second person in the European Community would favor environmental protection; only about one in ten would vote for industry; about one in three feel that both are equally important; and about one in ten are undecided. In the complete statistics, Spain has the most "don't knows," with one quarter of the population still undecided. Luxembourg has much more definite views with only 1 percent "don't knows" and the highest percentage coming down in favor of the environment. According to this survey, Ireland is the country with the strongest business support.

the many organizations that have emerged to address environment and business, its members include major companies such as Dow Chemical, AEG-UK, Leyland DAF, Prospect Foods, Baxi Heating, and such notable organizations as the Coventry Pollution Prevention Panel, the British Soft Drinks Association, and the Southampton Industrial Environmental Association. Membership includes not only large companies but also small and medium-sized enterprises in both manufacturing and service industries (e.g., consultants).

TREE UK is considering the development of specific programs for various sectors of the economy, for example, in collaboration with Leyland DAF for the automotive industry, or together with the British Soft Drinks Association for the beverage sector.

Denmark

ELM Denmark, *Erhvervslivets Ledelsesforum for Miljöfremme,* was created in August 1991 by a core group of Danish companies including the Danish National Railways (DSB), and led by Brodrene Hartmann, a world leader in molded fiber packaging. It presently has the following company members: Brodrene Hartmann, InvestMiljo, Danish National Railways, Renholdingsselskabet af 1898, Rendan, Jiffy, Ramboll & Hannemann, and Danapak.

ELM Denmark defines its goals as follows: to encourage companies' responsibilities toward the environment; to promote knowledge of the ideas of ELM in both trade and industry and among the general public; to continue the development of the integrated system of environmental management; to provide services to its members including exchange of information, members' meetings, conferences, and advisory services; to involve itself in other organizations, both domestic and international, with the purpose of promoting environmental management; and to act as a catalyst for environmental management.

Associations in Other Countries

Hong Kong

In Hong Kong, the Private Sector Committee on the Environment (PSCE) was created in December 1988 in the wake of a decision by some of Hong Kong's leading companies to explore a private sector approach to environmental issues. The PSCE aims to pool the resources of leading Hong Kong companies, to address pressing environmental problems, and to set an example for other operations. The companies include China Power & Light, Du Pont, the Hong Kong Bank, the Hong Kong Tourist Association, Hutchison Whampoa, ICI China, Jardine Pacific, Modern Terminals, Reuters, Shell Hong Kong, the South China Morning Post, the Swire Group, and Whard Holdings.

The PSCE has taken action toward the cleanup of the harbor, sponsoring an experiment to install screens at three outfalls, and funding a boat scavenging service. In addition, the PSCE is tackling the problem of Hong Kong's excessive waste disposal. Members have investigated the handling of their own companies' waste paper, and some are now arranging their own waste paper collection programs.

The PSCE has commissioned various studies, including one to assess the potential for exchange of waste materials in Hong Kong's electroplating sector, and others on ways to recover metals, acids, and other materials from the waste of local industry. It has addressed the issue of "Market Environmentalism: Lessons for Hong Kong," both in a publication and in presentations on the topic.

The PSCE is funding an environmental center whose main objective is the generation, marketing, and implementation of environmental projects that have a direct impact on Hong Kong's environment. The center's functions include the development and promotion of pollution control equipment; the provision of a pollution advisory service to industry; coordination and management of consultancies; management of a waste exchange scheme and a waste recycling information center; and marketing these services through seminars, publications, and publicity.

South Africa

The Industrial Environmental Forum (IEF) of Southern Africa was founded in August 1990 at the initiative of a number of major South African companies. It now has around fifty member companies from a cross section of South Africa's heavy industry and manufacturing industry (energy generation, iron and steel, coal and mining, cement, chemicals, paper, and the automotive industry). Its members include ESKOM, Caltex Oil, BP Southern Africa, Mobil, Chamber of Mines, Nissan, Toyota, Highveld Steel, Rand Mines, AECI Explosives and Chemicals, TransNatal Coal, Sappi Paper & Pulp, Sentrachem, South African Airways, and Pick'n Pay.

IEF is the only member organization of INEM that explicitly aims to go beyond the borders of its own country, working on a wider regional basis. This concept is tailored to the conditions of Southern Africa, and demonstrates the flexibility of the INEM member organizations. INEM intends to extend its cooperation with IEF to cover other countries in Southern Africa, to help interested companies develop their own organization for environmental management—as has already been done in Zimbabwe. The IEF action program includes the development of an environmental Code of Conduct for business and a systematic search to identify those areas where action is most urgently required. Further points in IEF's program are information procurement for the member companies and the organization of intercompany exchange of experience.

Further working groups will be established with specific goals (e.g., preparation of guidelines for eco-auditing) or informative character (e.g., clean air management). The secretariat helps to find qualified experts, mostly from among the member companies, to give lectures to working groups.

Japan

In Japan, the Eco-Life Center (originally named the Eco-Business Center) was created in June 1991 to foster environmental awareness in business, government, academic circles, and the general public, and to promote an environmentally more benign life-style in Japan. It currently has 131 corporate and individual members. The corporate members include CGC Japan, Doei Paper Industry, Chioda Bank, Co-op Japan, Dynax Urban Environmental Research Institute, Toyo Glass, and INAX.

The Eco-Life Center's activities include periodic members' meetings; creation of information sources on eco-business and eco-products; coordination of projects relating to environmental business; research and development of eco-products, distribution, sales, and so forth; planning and coordination of conferences, symposia, and tours; campaigns conducted jointly with the media, administration, and consumer groups to promote ecological life-styles in Japan; publication of guidebooks for eco-products and member organizations; coordination of the "Eco-Life and Business Network" meetings; and publication of magazines, newsletters, and books. The Eco-Life Center has cooperated with the Japan Environment Agency on the development of the Japanese eco-labeling system (Eco-Mark) and the Japanese Consumers' Cooperative Union on their Environment 21 project, which seeks to reorient the life-styles of its 14 million members to diminish their environmental impact.

Municipal governments in Tokyo, Kyoto, and Osaka have initiated recycling and substitution of tropical hardwood used for concrete molds in public construction projects. The initiatives were in response to growing public pressure about Japan's role in the destruction of rain forests led by JATAN (Japan Tropical Forest Action Network). The social and environmental corporate ratings published annually in the *Asahi Journal* are exposing more companies to ecological auditing as well as to public scrutiny.

The Valdez Society, named after the Valdez Principles (now called the CERES Principles), formed in May 1990. By October 1992 they had 200 members encompassing citizen activists, corporate employees, scholars, and journalists. Their first major publicity came from their attempt to rank companies' environmental performance.

The Valdez Society is comprised of three committees. The Green Consumer Group studies green consumerism to influence corporate marketing strategies and promotes ecologically sound markets. Their first annual report ranked fifty-one supermarket operators. The Socially Responsible Investment Group studies methods by which investors can improve corporate environmental practices. The Corporate Environmentalism Group, made up of company employees, researches management strategies that would prompt companies to improve environmental policies voluntarily (Tetsuro 1992).

Brazil

SIGA, the Society for the Promotion of Environmental Management (*Sociedade para o Incentivo ao Gerenciamento Ambiental*), is the first

B.A.U.M.-type association to be created in Latin America. It was launched in Rio on October 9, 1991, at the initiative of several business groups: GIE and Pro Rio in '92 in Rio, PNBE in São Paulo and companies such as João Fortes Engenharia (Rio) and the CETEST Group (São Paulo).

The importance of a Brazilian member of INEM is underscored by the United Nations Conference on Environment and Development, also known as the "Earth Summit" (June 3 to 14, 1992). The Brazilian experience may serve as a role model for other Latin American nations and other developing countries.

SIGA will also set up working groups, including one to help Brazilian companies find ways of using locally renewable resources to manufacture environmentally friendlier products.

Israel

In Israel, the ALVA—Society of Industry for Ecology—was created in January 1992, following the initiative of Ormat Industries, a biotechnological and alternative energy systems group, together with representatives of the Israeli Manufacturers Association, the Society for the Protection of Nature in Israel and the Ministry of the Environment, the Ministry of Industry and Trade, and other relevant ministries and authorities.

Zimbabwe

The Environmental Forum of Zimbabwe (EFZ), founded early in 1992, aims to promote responsible, self-regulatory environmental management in agricultural and mining industries, business, and commerce. Member organizations are expected to promote environmental management within their own structures, including complying with environmental legislation and adopting corporate environmental policies, such as environmental education and motivation of personnel. Members also exchange information and know-how among themselves.

In the next chapter we discuss some of the changes in thinking that underlie the new practices that companies mentioned above have pioneered.

4

THE PARADIGM SHIFT FROM ENVIRONMENTALISM TO ECOMANAGEMENT

To establish the conceptual framework for the theory and practice of ecomanagement, to be discussed in Part II, we shall now distinguish between "environmental management" and "ecological management" (or "ecomanagement"). We use the former term to refer to the defensive, reactive approach exemplified by reactive environmental efforts and compliance auditing; the latter to indicate the proactive, creative approach developed in Germany and refined conceptually by the Elmwood Institute. The purpose of ecomanagement is to minimize a company's environmental and social impact and make all its operations as ecologically sound as possible.

TRANSFORMING FROM ENVIRONMENTAL
TO ECOLOGICAL MANAGEMENT

Our starting point is the recognition that the world's ecological problems, like all the other major problems of our time, cannot be understood in isolation. They are systemic problems—interconnected and interdependent—and need a new kind of systemic, or ecological, thinking to be understood and solved (Lutz 1990, 3). Moreover, this new thinking must be accompanied by a shift in values from expansion to conservation, from quantity to quality, from domination to partnership. The new value system and thinking, together with corresponding new perceptions and practices, are what we call the "new paradigm" (see "Critical Questions About New Paradigm Thinking," *ReVision* 1986).

The philosophy underlying the practice of ecomanagement, as understood by Elmwood, is based on the conviction that the ecological impact of a company's operations will not improve significantly unless the company goes through a radical change in its corporate culture—a paradigm shift as described above. (To elucidate, promote, and facilitate this shift is the very purpose of the Elmwood Institute. To do so, the Institute makes a variety of resources available to its members—books, journals, newsletters, audio- and videotapes, discussion circles, and so forth.)

The new paradigm may be called a holistic worldview—seeing the world as an integrated whole rather than a dissociated collection of parts. It may be called a systemic view, or systems view, referring to its more abstract theoretical underpinning by systems theory. Finally, the new paradigm may be called an ecological view, using that term in a much broader and deeper sense than usual.

SHALLOW ENVIRONMENTALISM AND DEEP ECOLOGY

Our distinction between environmental management and ecological management implies the use of "ecological" in that broader and deeper sense. We see our terminology as a specific application of the distinction between "shallow environmentalism" and "deep ecology," terms coined in the 1970s by the Norwegian philosopher Arne Naess (Devall and Sessions 1985). This very useful terminology is now widely accepted in making this distinction and for understanding a major division within contemporary environmental thought.

In his review paper, "Deep Ecology: A New Philosophy of Our Time?", Warwick Fox (1984) discusses the following three characteristics of Arne Naess's distinction, each of which is clearly pertinent to our distinction between (shallow) environmental and (deep) ecological management.

> *Shallow environmentalism accepts the dominant mechanistic paradigm. Deep ecology involves the shift to a holistic, systemic worldview.*

Environmental auditing and other environmental management practices do not question the dominant corporate paradigm. They see the company as a machine that can be controlled and they adopt the framework of conventional economics. In compliance auditing, methods based purely on quantification can be applied, since government regulations and standards are quantified. However, this necessarily reinforces the status quo and offers no guidance for solving urgent environmental problems not reflected in governmental actions.

Ecomanagement involves the shift from mechanistic to systemic thinking. An essential aspect of this shift is a change in perception from the world as machine to the world as a living system. This change concerns our perception of nature, of the human organism, of society, and thus also our perception of a business organization. Companies are living systems that cannot be workably comprehended from the economic point of view alone. As a living system, the company cannot be rigidly controlled through direct intervention but can be influenced by conveying orientations and giving impulses. Such a new style of management is known as systemic management (Capra, Exner, and Königswieser n.d.).

> *Shallow environmentalism is anthropocentric: it views humans as the source of all value and ascribes only use value to nature. Deep ecology recognizes the intrinsic values of all living beings and views humans as just one particular strand in the web of life.*

Environmental management is associated with the idea of coping with environmental problems for the benefit of the company. It lacks an ethical dimension and its main motivations are legal compliance and improvement of the corporate image. Ecomanagement, by contrast, is motivated by an ecological ethic and by a concern for the well-being of future generations. Its starting point is a change of values within the corporate culture.

> *Shallow environmentalism tends to either accept by default or positively endorse the ideology of economic growth. Deep ecology replaces the ideology of economic growth with the idea of ecological sustainability.*

Deep ecological thinking generates a number of possibilities. Companies could decide to stop producing and receiving packaging within two years, for example. Companies—whether manufacturing toxic agricultural pesticides exported to the developing world or petroleum-based sequined dresses sewn by child labor in sweatshops—can develop strategies to invest in research to develop substitutes, replace the products and practices with others, or prepare to phase out of the business entirely within a set period of time if the other solutions cannot be found.

Today, shallow environmentalism is evidenced as "greenwashing," a practice in which companies make cosmetic environmental changes for cynical public relations purposes. These companies spend money on "green" advertising, marketing, and corporate image-enhancing, but not on "greening" production processes, facilities, and employee working conditions. Such practices can also reflect corporate ignorance about possible ecological change. Concerned corporate planners are often genuinely stymied about how to integrate an ecological approach when faced with conflicting demands from competing stakeholders, particularly stockholders, whose expectations focus on quarterly profit statements. Opting only for a simple recycling or energy-efficiency program (important and useful efforts in their own right), rather than going on to a fundamental reevaluation of products and production processes, can seem satisfactory to a manager who has not heard of the innovations made by other companies.

Environmental auditing does not question the ideology of economic growth, which is the main driving force of current economic policies and, tragically, of global environmental destruction. Rejecting this ideology does not mean rejecting all growth, but rather rejecting the blind pursuit of *unrestricted* economic growth, understood in purely quantitative terms as maximization of profits or the GNP. Ecological auditing includes the recognition that unlimited economic growth on a finite planet can only lead to disaster. Accordingly, the concept of growth is qualified by introducing ecological sustainability as a key criterion for all business activities.

How difficult it is sometimes to distinguish between deep ecological transformation and shallow environmentalism is shown with the debate about Du Pont. Du Pont advertised its performance goals for the year 2000 and publicized its good intentions with its oil-company subsidiary Conoco (double-hull tankers, for example). After a systematic assessment in 1990, Du Pont began investing nearly $1 billion a year in reducing toxic emissions on the determination that it was cheaper to redesign for zero toxic waste than to continue exposure to litigation by carrying out only incremental pollution reduction.

It must be noted, however, that Du Pont is still one of America's top corporate polluters, releasing 350 million pounds of toxics into the environment each year. There is obviously a deep gap remaining between "corporate environmentalism" and achieving a thorough-going transformation of the company.

Pioneer and Mainstream Companies

Pioneer companies, of which Patagonia, the outdoor clothing manufacturer, is an example, have managements with an environmentally or socially responsible worldview. They tend to be privately owned and small to middle-sized (under $400 million). A founder is often still closely involved in running the company. They are often newer companies that have experienced growth for the bulk of their life spans. Many of these companies are in service industries or disposable consumer goods: ice cream, cosmetics, specialty clothing, specialty entertainment.

Mainstream companies, of which Du Pont is an example, may not be driven by deep ecology, but they tend to have stronger management experience. These companies are accustomed to strategic planning, long-range scenario development, total quality management, and in-depth market analysis. They often have more resources to invest in ecological innovation, although they face harsher constraints. Mainstreamers represent the vast majority of publicly held companies and the majority of "essential" industry: food, clothing, construction, energy, transportation, communication, industrial materials, and so forth. Mainstream companies also represent the industries most under environmental pressure. According to Dr. Martin Holdgate, Director General of the World Conservation Union (Elkington and Dimmock 1992), these companies are

- Most responsible for greenhouse gases or ozone depletion (e.g., energy, solvents)
- Undertaking massive manipulations of the natural environment (e.g., mining, oil, timber)
- Licensed to discharge specific quantities of pollutants, but face tightening regulations (e.g., pharmaceuticals, metals processing, pesticides)

Pioneer companies can be disdainful of the difficulties in changing essential industries from which society depends on a consistent supply of familiar, staple products. In the publicly held American company, managers' job evaluations can rest on delivering favorable quarterly reports to shareholders, which institutionalizes resistance to costly, longer-term change. Mainstream companies can be complacent, looking toward incremental improvement rather than transformation for sustainability. They often think pioneers are ecological dreamers who cannot possibly appreciate the constraints of running a "serious" business. Pioneers, on the other hand, may think of mainstreamers as carrying a bigger responsibility to change because they've made a bigger mess.

A mainstream company's motivation for change may be purely pragmatic: risk management, strategic planning, competitive positioning, or profiting in new consumer markets. While ecological transformation may not have provided the impetus, its ecomanagement practices can be as strong or stronger than those of the pioneer. It is essential to look carefully at what companies do, not what they say they do. Large-scale ecological capital investment can commit a company to intensive ecological change, regardless of stated beliefs.

Pioneer companies are motivated toward ecological change because of their management's worldview. They often shoot from the hip in their founder's entrepreneurial style. It can be difficult for such companies to maintain deep ecomanagement efforts when facing economic downturns or intensified competition. They may miss the human dimension of the effort and presume that people who don't adhere to their worldview (both employees and outside stakeholders) are not to be trusted, rather than see them as potential allies.

Pioneer and mainstream companies often show dramatic contrasts in organizational cultures, hinging on such symbols as dress norms (T-shirt and jeans versus three-piece suits) and corporate social activities (camping trips versus golf resorts). Those visible cues do not always match the actions of the two types of companies. A pioneer company may have an excellent recycling program, but pay low wages, bust unions, and offer no health care benefits for employees and their families. A mainstream company may invest in groundbreaking research on and development of ecologically innovative products while deciding that the relative cost of fines versus cleanup justifies violation of EPA regulations in the short run.

Stronger lines of communication between pioneer and mainstream companies can help break down stereotypes, strengthen alliances for ecomanagement, and enable each group to learn from the strengths of the other. Both groups are needed to shepherd the efforts of new ventures or companies hovering on the brink of change. Every type of company needs to be welcomed into ecomanagement networks that will both facilitate and intensify the shift to an ecological world view in both theory and practice.

Diversity and EcoManagement

An ecomanagement perspective ensures that environmental and social concerns do not compete. If social, labor, or cultural issues seem to conflict with the environmental agenda, the company is on the wrong track. The ecomanager must be prepared for the challenge of finding the bridges between the concerns.

People of color, women, labor, and other groups affected differently by company actions can be the ecomanager's best allies in bringing unique insights and solutions to problems. Ecological transformation is limited and likely to prove fragile without diverse participation, perspectives, and bases of support.

No one wants to be a token. Build diverse perspectives into the planning process from the beginning. Make sure that not only one person is expected to represent "minorities," but that there is the support of more than one person from previously underrepresented groups. Ask the entire group to consider diversity issues rather than delegating those concerns only to the individual of that culture.

Take the extra time for diverse representation at the beginning. It is difficult to garner buy-in for change after all the decisions have been made. It may take more time to recruit people who have not been associated with environmental concerns or management issues, but people will be more invested in ensuring the success of an effort they help shape. The extra time will pay off in sounder strategy, leadership that can better mobilize different stakeholders, credibility for the effort, and depth that only comes from acting on principles, "walking the talk."

Elmwood's Definition of an Eco-Audit

Based on the preceding discussion of the differences between (shallow) environmental and (deep) ecological auditing, we shall adopt the following definition of an eco-audit:

> *An eco-audit, as understood by the Elmwood Institute, is an examination and review of a company's operations from the perspective of deep ecology, or the new paradigm. It is motivated by a shift in values within the corporate culture from domination to partnership, from the ideology of economic growth to that of ecological sustainability. It involves a corresponding shift from mechanistic to systemic thinking and, accordingly, a new style of management known as systemic management. The result of the eco-audit is an action plan for minimizing the*

company's environmental impact and making all its operations more ecologically sound.

The term "audit," derived of course from financial audits, tends to connote a precise and narrowly defined examination according to government regulations, company policies, or "generally accepted practices." Eco-auditing in the broad sense, as advocated by Elmwood, includes procedures that are sometimes called surveys, assessments, appraisals, reviews, and so on. The common element in these terms is an indication that a systematic examination of a company's operations, from an ecological standpoint, is being carried out.

It is important to note that since the employees who actually do the work are the most familiar with it, they must be part of the audit procedures. They are likely to come up with many innovative ideas, given suitable genuine encouragement and reward; thus, one "methodology" for ecological improvement in a company is to mobilize the concern and ingenuity of all employees. The capacity of the audit to transform company practices proves most effective when the process of conducting the audit itself models the kind of systemic, ecological company practices that are ultimately sought.

PART II

THEORY AND PRACTICE OF ECOMANAGEMENT

5

MANAGING THE CHANGE TO AN ECOLOGICALLY CONSCIOUS CORPORATE CULTURE

Our starting point is the conviction that ecomanagement involves basic changes in the corporate culture. Ecomanagement, and the eco-audit itself as understood by Elmwood, are motivated by the values and based upon the concept of deep ecology. Their success will depend on the extent to which the ecological paradigm is reflected in the corporate culture. (The first six chapters of Part II draw heavily from Georg Winter et al., *Das umweltbewußte Unternehmen* [1987], and to some extent from the English version, *Business and the Environment* [1989].)

NEW PERCEPTIONS, IDEAS, AND VALUES

The concepts of "paradigm" and "corporate culture" are closely related. A social paradigm may be defined (see "Critical Questions" 1986) as a constellation of concepts, values, perceptions, and practices, shared by a community, which forms a particular vision of reality that then becomes the basis for the way a community organizes itself. Corporate culture may be defined as a cohesion of ideas, values, norms, and modes of conduct, which has been accepted and adopted by a company through a process of consensus, and which constitutes the distinctive, unmistakable character of the organization. Or, as the managing director of a major consulting company put it more informally, corporate culture is "the way we do things around here" (Deal and Kennedy 1982, 4).

The basic question, then, is: What does it mean to expand and redefine the corporate culture in such a way that it reflects the paradigm of deep ecology? It would go far beyond the scope of this book to discuss the paradigm shift in science and society in all its ramifications. In the following paragraphs we shall merely outline the key elements of the change of paradigms, with special emphasis on those most relevant to the corresponding redefinition of corporate culture.

An ecologically conscious company has a corporate culture that embraces distinct perceptions, ideas, values, and behaviors. A successful eco-audit can identify which of the following understandings need greater awareness.

State of the World

The nineties are a critical decade. The survival of humanity and of the planet are at stake. We are faced with a series of global problems that are harming the biosphere and human life in alarming ways that may soon become irreversible (see Worldwatch Institute's annual *State of the World* reports). The Earth's forests are being cut down, while its deserts are expanding. Topsoil on our croplands is diminishing, and the ozone layer, which protects us from harmful ultraviolet radiation, is being depleted. Concentrations of heat-trapping gases in the atmosphere are rising, while numbers of wild plant and animal species are shrinking. World population continues to grow, and the gap between the rich and poor continues to widen.

Interconnectedness of Problems

None of these problems can be understood in isolation. They are systemic problems—interconnected and interdependent—and need a systemic approach to be understood and solved.

Shift from Objects to Relationships

The systemic nature of the world's problems derives from the fact that the world itself, our planet Earth, is an integrated whole, a living system. The shift of perception from the world as a machine to the world as a living system is a key characteristic of the ecological paradigm. Reality is no longer seen as a collection of separate objects but rather as an inseparable web of relationships.

Shift from the Parts to the Whole

Living systems comprise individual organisms, social systems, and ecosystems, all of which are integrated wholes embedded in larger wholes on which they depend. Systemic properties are destroyed when a system is dissected, either physically or theoretically, into isolated elements. Although we can discern individual parts in any system, the nature of the whole is always different from the mere sum of the parts. The nature of any living system, including a business organization, derives from the relationships among its components and from the relationships of the whole system to its environment.

Shift from Domination to Partnership

The shift of values from domination to partnership is another key element of the ecological paradigm (Eisler 1987). Whereas a machine is properly understood through domination and control, the understanding of a living system will be much more successful if approached through cooperation and partnership. In nature, all competition is intricately connected with cooperation. Cooperative, symbiotic relationships are an essential characteristic of the web of life.

Shift from Structures to Processes

Systems thinking is process thinking. Every structure is a manifestation of underlying processes. The web of relationships is intrinsically dynamic. Fluctuations play a crucial role. The system's stability is achieved through a dynamic balance, characterized by continual interdependent fluctuations of all variables. The more dynamic the state of balance, the more flexible the living system; the more flexible the system, the greater its stability. Stress is the lack of flexibility.

Shift from Self-Assertion to Integration

A healthy dynamic balance in living systems includes the balance between self-assertion and integration, two essential tendencies of all life. As integral wholes, living systems need to assert themselves in their individuality; as part of larger wholes, they need to integrate themselves into the larger patterns. In our culture we have overemphasized self-assertion—competition, expansion, quantity—and neglected integration—cooperation, conservation, quality. The paradigm shift includes the shift in values from self-assertion toward integration.

Shift from Growth to Sustainability

As far as business organizations are concerned, the most important example of the shift from expansion to conservation, from quantity to quality, is the shift in fundamental criteria of "success" from economic growth to ecological sustainability. As mentioned before, the blind pursuit of unrestricted growth is the main driving force of global environmental destruction. Growth, of course, is characteristic of all life. In the living world, however, growth has not only a quantitative meaning. Ecologically conscious management includes qualifying economic growth by also introducing sustainability as a key criterion for all business activities. What is sustained in a living system over time is its pattern of organization, that is, the web of relationships that defines the system as an integrated whole. That pattern, the very essence of the system, is a qualitative feature.

SYSTEMIC MANAGEMENT

Corporate culture is the result of a long process of consensus, and any changes in it will require the involvement of people at all levels of the company's organizational structure. Although top management sanction is critical to consistent, deep corporate change, ecological consensus cannot be imposed from on high. It must be developed creatively with the inner commitment of the entire work force. This is why the practice of "systemic management" must be an integral part of ecomanagement. This new style of leadership, informed by systemic thinking and acting, has been developed in Europe over the last decade. It is now also gaining acceptance in the United States. We shall limit ourselves here to a few key points.

Systemically oriented managers do not see themselves as the dominators and controllers within the company, but rather as "cultivators" or "catalysts." Being aware of the nature of the company as a living system, they give "impulses" rather than instructions.

Systemic managers have to learn how to live with uncertainty. They act within a social system which they cannot comprehend completely and whose reactions and events they will never predict with certainty, let alone control. This does not relieve them, however, from the responsibility for providing guidance to the organization.

The view of the stability and flexibility of a social system as a consequence of its dynamic balance suggests a corresponding strategy of conflict resolution. In every company, as in society as a whole, conflicts and contradictions will invariably appear that cannot be simply resolved in favor of one or the other side. Thus, we need stability and change, order and freedom, tradition and innovation, planning and laissez-faire.

A systemically oriented manager knows that the contradictions within a company are signs of its variety and vitality, and thus contribute to the system's viability. Without conflicts there can be no development. A systemic manager will therefore try to take into account both sides of a contradiction, knowing that both will be important depending on the context. He or she will try to solve inevitable conflicts not by means of rigid decisions but rather through dynamically balancing both sides.

CORPORATE GOALS AND STRATEGIES

Critical Analysis of Corporate Philosophy

The first step in redefining the company's corporate culture will be a critical analysis of its corporate philosophy: To what extent are the perceptions, ideas, and values outlined in the beginning of this chapter reflected in the corporate culture? Such a critical analysis might begin with very general and deep questions. The top managers will need to ask themselves in all honesty:

- Am I really concerned about the state of the world, or will I merely act to give myself a better image or boost my ego?
- Do I really understand the key ideas of ecology, or do I merely repeat a few buzzwords?
- Do I myself live in an ecologically conscious way, or is there a discrepancy between my words and my acts? Do I "walk my talk"?
- To what extent are the principles of systemic management part of our corporate culture?

The next step might be to examine the ecological sustainability of the industry of which the company is a part:

- Are the products and services of the industry ecologically sound, or are they unnecessarily destructive?
- What changes would make the industry less ecologically damaging?

Then the sustainability of the company might be examined:

- What is our philosophy regarding economic growth?
- How would we qualify the concept of growth?
- Can we remain motivated to change without the goal of quantitative growth?

A thorough examination of these basic philosophical questions may lead to an expansion, or reformulation, of the company's mission statement to reflect deep ecological values.

Analysis of Key Issues

The preceding philosophical analysis should allow reformulation of corporate goals and strategies in such a way that they include the ecological dimension as an integral part. To begin, it will be useful to focus on key ecological issues in the company's areas of activity.

What are the *opportunities* and *risks* in our operating environment and in the market?

- Legislation
- Public awareness

- Customers' awareness
- Competitors' activities
- Scientific and technological developments

What are our *strengths* or *weaknesses?*

- Availability of finances for ecologically oriented investments
- Ecological awareness of top management
- Flexibility of management and staff
- Relevance of the company's products and services to environmental protection and social justice
- Support of the community for ecological improvements

Formulating Ecologically Oriented Corporate Goals

Once the key ecological issues have been identified and analyzed, ecologically oriented corporate goals may be formulated. It may be helpful to begin this process by formulating a set of *ecological guiding principles,* such as the following:

- Demonstrate compatibility of market economy with ecological requirements
- Safeguard the company's survival by recognizing global trends at an early stage and planning accordingly
- Seek competitive advantages by minimizing environmental impacts
- Adopt a proactive, creative approach to ecological challenges in all areas of the company's activity
- Cooperate with business and academic partners to speed up the accumulation of ecological knowledge

The *long-term ecological goals* for the company as a whole may then be formulated, such as:

- Capitalize on the goodwill of staff, the general public, and government agencies resulting from the company's ecological commitment

- Take advantage of cost cutting through energy and resource conservation and progress in other ecofriendly technologies
- Minimize risks arising from management or product liabilities, sudden changes in legal norms, or sudden increases in ecologically motivated consumer demands
- Influence legislation through ecologically oriented lobbying

Similar goals need to be formulated for all *departments*. For example:

- Personnel: increase the company's attractiveness to environmentally concerned employees, thus reinforcing staff loyalty
- Procurement: manifest ecological awareness in purchase of raw materials and supplies
- Production: cut costs by saving energy, raw materials, and water
- Product design: revise specifications to lessen impacts in production, use, and disposal
- Distribution: seek to use means of transportation that expend less energy and cause less pollution

Finally, the relationships between the company's ecological and economic goals need to be assessed:

- Analyze implications of ecological goals for turnover, costs, and profits
- Identify major areas of conflict
- Lay down long-term priorities within the system of corporate goals, possibly with ecological priorities changing over time

MOTIVATING CHANGE

Change toward ecologically responsible operations depends on the participation of everyone in a company. Any members of the management team who are not convinced of the need for and advantages of ecologically conscious management must first be motivated. As long as the employees are not convinced, the project will fail no matter how well it has been prepared in other respects.

Formulating and implementing the corporate goals and strategies discussed in the preceding section will be much easier if the management style is cooperative and systemic. The focus should be on liberating people's energies; recognizing their latent potentials; giving orientations; setting processes in motion; showing respect and consideration; emphasizing intuition, meaning, and vision; increasing flexibility; and enhancing the system's learning potential. Once these patterns are established, the eco-auditing project may virtually run itself.

Convincing department heads of the advantage of an eco-audit will be much more effective if you emphasize their own department's concerns, using examples to highlight the point. For example, emphasize human relations with the head of personnel; publicity, image, and advertising with the head of sales; reducing waste disposal problems with the head of materials management; and cost savings with the head of finance.

It will also help to appeal to whatever personally motivates the department heads, empathizing with their feelings and thought processes. Where there is a perceptible desire to enhance the corporate spirit, mention the integrating effect of ecological consciousness; where there is an evident need for public esteem, stress removing the blemish of environmental damage caused by certain company activities; where there is a pressing need for self-realization, focus on the opportunity to do genuine pioneer work in the area where economics and ecology meet.

When it comes to making decisions, individuals should be well prepared. Provide information and motivate people in advance. If the decision is likely to be controversial, possibly wait for an opportune moment, for example, the announcement of a successful year's sales, a special anniversary, or a major order.

When the decision has been made, it will be wise to give special attention to those members of the management team who were outvoted, rather than treat them as defeated opponents.

Decisions on ecological measures should be given wide in-house publicity to ensure that the management team is seen to be acting in unison and to bind its individual members more strongly to the collective decision. When the decision generates positive responses and results, all those involved in it should be acknowledged, both in the company and in the media, so that everyone may share in the success. When there is a negative response (e.g., carping about the quality of recycled paper), stand by the members of the recycling team who are under fire to strengthen the team spirit. Every opportunity should be taken to thank and praise members of the team for their ecological awareness, thus motivating others for future actions.

The strongest motivating force for the company's people will be their sense of personal integrity and significant involvement in the firm. As ecological awareness rises among the general public, employees will increasingly feel that they can no longer fully identify with environmentally destructive jobs. The more they realize that their work will contribute to protecting the environment, the more enthusiastic they will become for carrying out the company's eco-audit and implementing its results.

It is also important to foster the awareness that high ecological standards go hand in hand with high standards of work in the traditional sense. By realizing that the shift from quantity to quality is a key characteristic of deep ecology, the new ecological consciousness may be integrated with traditional concerns for high-quality work. Similar considerations apply to the quality of human relationships within the company, the physical working environment, food, and so on. The more humane, healthy and ecologically sound these are, the easier it will be to raise ecological consciousness.

As with managers, it will help to appeal to employees' personal concerns and motivations. For example, the need for safety may be addressed by improved safety information and monitoring; the need for a sense of belonging by leading and participating in educational group activities; the need for material rewards by bonuses and other incentives; the need for status by awards and other signs of recognition; and the need for self-realization by increased participation in ecological planning and strategizing.

Since the ecological paradigm involves a holistic view of the world and of human nature, it will also be useful to address the whole person in motivation and training programs. This may involve addressing feelings through an experiential approach to ecology, through training in systems thinking; addressing the sense of responsibility by emphasizing responsibility for one's health, one's fellow human beings, other living creatures, and future generations; addressing judgment by developing the ability to assess and select ecological options; and addressing action through constant encouragement to put new insights and decisions into practice.

In all these areas, psychological preparation, moral support, and the rewarding of success will be crucial. No one should be presented with a fait accompli. Employees should participate in and be consulted well in advance of any decision, so that their expertise is acknowledged and utilized. Thanks and praise for successful ecological measures need to be given generously.

Having made these general comments, we shall now list some suggestions for developing a coherent employee motivation and training scheme. Four basic questions need to clarified:

- Who is to be motivated and trained?
- Who is to be responsible for motivation and training?
- What is to be conveyed?
- Which methods are likely to be successful?

People to be motivated and trained may include trainees; employees' families, household members, and domestic partners; and employees of service companies who work regularly or frequently in the company.

People responsible for motivation and training may include, in addition to in-house executives and environmental officers, representatives of environmental agencies; scientists, engineers, and inventors; representatives of environmental organizations, unions, and consumer associations; representatives of companies producing environmental technologies; craftspeople who practice their crafts in ecologically sound ways and are able to give practical demonstrations; and public figures and celebrities who can speak about ecological principles or their own ecological commitment and thus set an example.

The perceptions, ideas, and values to be conveyed have been previously outlined. The basic insights are not difficult to understand, and they convey an exciting new way of seeing the world. The more all employees comprehend and embrace them, the stronger will be the collective motivation for ecologically sound business operations.

Over the past decade, a great variety of *motivation and training methods* have been used successfully, both in Europe and the United States. The examples listed below should allow each company to select methods most appropriate to its own corporate culture.

Dissemination of Information

Notice boards, the company newspaper, circulated material, an ecology library, regular reports, and speeches for special occasions are all effective channels to disseminate ecological information.

- *Bulletin boards* may display press articles dealing with the environment, information on forthcoming radio and television programs, and information on in-house ecological measures. A special "ecology notice board" would emphasize the extension of the company's goals into this new domain.

- The *company newsletter* could feature a regular environment column, a special issue on the environment, and special issues on ecological life-styles (recycling, organic gardening, bicycling, etc.).

- *Circulated material* on environmental issues may include material published by the Worldwatch Institute, Greenpeace, and other environmental organizations.

- A special *ecology library* could include books, magazines, newsletters, charts, posters, slides, audio and video cassettes.

- *Regular reports* and the traditional *speeches for special occasions* offer ideal opportunities to report on successes and shortcomings in the company's ecological management and to demonstrate that it is an integral part of corporate policy.

Social Events

In addition to speeches at the traditional social functions, special events may be created to promote ecological awareness. These might include:

- An environmental raffle at office parties with a bicycle as the main prize and ecologically oriented books, videotapes, and so on as additional prizes
- Bicycle excursions or nature walks for employees
- Visits to ecological showplaces: demonstration houses, efficient companies, alternative energy installations and so forth
- Open house days for employees and their families, domestic partners, and friends to demonstrate the company's ecological practices
- A party for employees and their families and friends to extend ecological awareness

Open house days, children's parties, and other events will be especially effective if residents in the neighborhood are invited as well. Particularly in small communities, this will have a very beneficial effect on the company's public image and may attract reporters from the local media.

Staff Involvement

All people in the company should be inspired and empowered to look for cost-cutting ecological measures, and successes should be rewarded. Before the beginning of each fiscal year, designated staff members in their departments should prepare a list of realistic ecological objectives for the year. These objectives should be discussed carefully before they are finalized to see whether they are consistent with the company's philosophy and with the departmental objectives. The checklists in Chapters 7–10 will be helpful for drawing up the list of objectives.

Special care should be taken to ensure that ecological and economic objectives are worked out with the same degree of thoroughness and that employees are equally determined to attain them.

Periodic interviews and progress reports might be considered, and the importance of replacing hierarchical monitoring with self-monitoring should be emphasized to increase staff involvement and job satisfaction.

Members of quality circles—in which employees make suggestions for improvements in a creative atmosphere without regard to hierarchical levels—should be encouraged to address themselves to ecological issues. Ecological consciousness is an integral part of quality consciousness.

Incentives

In all incentive schemes great care must be taken to ensure that the criteria on which rewards are based are clearly defined and equitably applied. Special incentives for ecological measures might include:

- A bonus for attaining or exceeding ecological objectives, designed in such a way that undertarget ecological performances cannot be offset by overtarget economic performances and vice versa

- A bonus scheme whereby the bonus for attaining economic objectives is reduced unless the ecological objectives are attained as well

- A company suggestion scheme for ecological measures that gives employees a share of the savings made as a result of their suggestions

- Nonmonetary rewards for ecological suggestions that will not save money

- Integration of ecological performance and economic performance in the company's promotion criteria

Recognition

Praise, thanks, and recognition for demonstrating ecological awareness are most appropriately expressed at public occasions and traditional social functions. Employees who have distinguished themselves may be given special awards at those occasions. Care should be taken that exceptional performances in the ecological domain and in traditional fields are rewarded in the same way. Job descriptions, compensation, and promotion criteria should be rewritten to credit effective participation on eco-teams and other ecologically oriented projects.

Employees who have distinguished themselves by originating or implementing ecological measures might also be suggested for awards by outside organizations. Moreover, effective public relations work should ensure that reports on the company's ecological activities appear in the media to give staff a feeling of recognition and strengthen the team spirit.

Support for Outside Environmental Projects

To create staff support for environmental projects outside the company, an environmental fund, made up of small voluntary contributions by staff members (matched or exceeded by company funds), may be set up. The fund should be managed jointly by staff and management.

Consider allowing environmental organizations to use specialized corporate facilities (such as specialized information networks) and to draw on employees' skills. This might include paid staff time for assisting in ecological projects.

Extension of Training

All training programs of the company will need to be extended to include the ecological dimension. This is especially important in the training of new employees, since they tend to be particularly receptive to ecological ideas and, being the new generation, will shape society in the future. A careful balance between economic and ecological effects should be established and maintained in all aspects of the training program. In particular, the misconception that the ecological component is a "soft option" should be eradicated. It should be made clear from the start of the program that the complexity of ecological interconnectedness poses difficulties but, at the same time, the resolution of ecological problems is especially rewarding.

Where a company maintains a major internal training program or participates in community adult training and continued-education

programs, it should foster a balance between conventional and ecological teaching.

- Ecological training must not degenerate into a separate
  course with no obvious links to occupational training;
  it needs to be an essential aspect of normal training
  courses.

- The ecological components of regular courses must not
  be combined into isolated "learning units." Employees
  need to be made aware of the ecological consequences of
  every work step and receive practical training so as to
  optimize the ecological aspects of each step.

- The ecological components must be integrated in two
  dimensions: horizontally, by ensuring that all operational
  aspects are considered from the ecological perspective;
  and vertically, by ensuring that each work step or process
  in a particular sector is assessed from the ecological point
  of view.

- Special care should be taken to train the training super-
  visors, and especially the master craftspeople, who often
  combine honesty with pride in their craft and a strong
  sense of responsibility.

- Full use should be made of the services offered by existing institutions—representatives of environmental organizations, environmental courses at university extensions
  and other institutions of adult education, correspon-
  dence courses, and so forth.

THE ORGANIZATION OF ECOMANAGEMENT

Many large companies have established environmental management
departments. These departments generally report to the first level
below the Chief Executive Officer (CEO) and are responsible for carrying out policies adopted by top management. This gives them the
organizational position they need to gain the serious attention of line
managers. Some organizational analysts believe, however, that large
line departments should also have their own environmental expertise

and that change can sometimes be introduced more effectively through such an arrangement.

Some companies utilize "technical committees" whose members are drawn from all departments, to ensure that ecological concerns are addressed everywhere in the company; such committees should be set up on an ongoing basis, hold regular meetings, and prepare periodic reports. It appears that different corporate cultures determine which arrangement will be best for different companies. The objective remains the same: to diffuse ecological attitudes throughout the company in a coordinated manner.

The role and duties of ecological managers should be clearly defined and well publicized within the company. A good deal of such managers' work will be done in collaboration with representatives from many company departments on various levels; sometimes companywide advisory committees are formed to assist the ecological manager. Some basic components of the positions include responsibility to:

- Manage programs to minimize waste emissions and comply with regulations
- Manage programs to minimize use of energy and water
- Assist in and help coordinate conversion to more ecologically acceptable products
- Prepare balance sheets that estimate as quantitatively as possible the benefits and costs of ecological programs within the company
- Monitor developments in ecological thinking and government environmental policies, giving early warning of implications for the company
- Monitor new products available for company procurement that are less ecologically damaging than ones presently used
- Handle liaison with unions regarding ecological matters
- Participate in ecological committees in the community and make recommendations for company positions and actions with regard to public issues

- Carry out information and training programs within the company, including meetings to educate employees and obtain feedback, tours of facilities, and so on
- Represent the company and its ecological policies to the community, bioregion, and outside world generally

It is of course critical that ecological managers be given the funds and other resources necessary to carry out these tasks. A second requirement is that where disagreements arise between the ecological manager and line departments, they should be decided without delay. (Top management must recognize that such conflicts are usually a positive sign, indicating that the ecological manager is doing her or his job of raising neglected issues and attempting to bring about change.)

Budgeting for ecological management requires top management to make difficult judgments about long-range benefits to the company, both internally and externally, and to the world at large. Investment for ecological purposes should be planned separately, and regular assessment of its effects should be carried out. A budget for ecological activities outside the company (membership in associations, grants to organizations, support for university or other research programs, publications, etc.) should be set up separately from general public relations funding.

When an ecological management department is first being set up, and auditing activities are being planned, it is important to include coverage of all departments, all subsidiaries, and all subcontractors or suppliers, since only in this way can accurate information about the impact of the company's activities be obtainable.

It is helpful to conclude audits with very specific goals and timetables for ecological improvement within the company—for example, to eliminate risks from storage or handling of hazardous substances within a few weeks, to reduce water consumption by 20 percent within six months, or to switch from certain problematic materials to less damaging ones within twelve months. Such goals must be communicated clearly and forcefully to all involved in achieving them, and completion of the goals should be appropriately recognized.

Some companies, in Scandinavia especially, have created the

position of "ombudsman" or "ombudsperson," who is charged with advising and representing employees outside the normal management and union channels. The existence of such a function, which in ecological matters would usually involve "whistle-blowing" employees, can contribute to the company's stability and its public image by reassuring employees, the surrounding community, and regulatory agencies.

EXPRESSION: ADVERTISING POLICY, PRODUCT DESIGN CRITERIA, PUBLIC IMAGE

The social/psychological context in which business now operates has been markedly changed by widespread public familiarity with ecological ideas. This has occurred in Western Europe, North America, and Japan. Eco-catastrophes, such as the Valdez oil spill, are reported with images diffused worldwide through modern media; these arouse short-term peaks of distaste for corporations and corporate executives. Clear-cuts of timber, air and water pollution, and landfill leakage problems have led to heavily negative public perceptions of industry as irresponsible or uncaring about the environment, and thus indirectly about people and their children.

This situation poses new problems for corporations' ways of presenting themselves to the world. Techniques of media "damage control" have not proved markedly effective; 25 percent of American consumers claim to have changed their buying choices because of negative impressions of particular companies. Thus, many companies have been seeking positive ways of portraying themselves. Various industries, seeking to justify practices that have come under criticism, have developed sizable public relations organizations. A good many corporations have sought to develop a more positive image by providing grants to environmental groups, though this practice can backfire if the groups begin to be seen as captive or dependent. Others have devoted research or community-relations resources to the solution of particular ecological problems.

These efforts, if honestly carried out, probably help to reduce open public criticism and political pressure for regulatory action; it is as yet unknown whether they will affect deeper public attitudes. However, since they are "cosmetic" and do not substantially affect the actual impact of corporate operations on the environment, they do not constitute a realistic or sufficient long-term adjustment to changing social conditions. For that, changes in the technical operating factors dealt with in eco-audits will be essential, including changes in the process of product design.

Since not long after World War II, product design in American companies has been largely driven by the sales department; and decorative or style aspects of goods have been emphasized, both in design and in advertising. Considerations such as engineering finesse, reliability, durability, and repairability have been given more emphasis by foreign producers, especially the Japanese; the favorable consumer response is manifested in the dimensions of the U.S. trade deficit. Only recently have companies begun to pay attention to ecological criteria for product design, and this mainly in Western Europe.

Large numbers of American consumers are already seeking assurance that the products they buy are the least ecologically damaging possible: recycled papers, low-energy-consumption appliances, and so on. These demands have not yet been significantly absorbed by the design profession. It is likely that in the next few years, however, corporations whose products stress features of ecological "safety," low impact, and a long lifetime of reliable use will be strongly favored by a large proportion of consumers, simply through the spread of "conserving" life-styles and ideas.

Moreover, this process will be accentuated as eco-labeling of products spreads from Western Europe throughout the other advanced countries. Through specific symbols printed on goods (see Figure 5 below), eco-labels will increasingly guide consumers

Fig. 5.   Sample Product Eco-labels

toward the purchase of less damaging products. Such labels state that a product (compared to other similar products) is, for example, made from recycled materials, consumes less energy or water, produces less air or water pollution, is less noisy, does not pose a contamination problem in use or disposal, or is free of such toxics as chlorine and lead. (For details, see Callenbach 1990.)

It is likely, therefore, that advertising policies will also have to adapt to changing conditions. "Image" advertising will have to become increasingly specific and concrete, to overcome chronic public skepticism fed by active media reporting in the environmental field. Product advertising should stress (1) lasting buyer satisfactions rather than transient ones; (2) attractive lifetime costs of products, rather than just initial costs (while ignoring operating or disposal costs); (3) competitive reliability, durability, and trouble-free qualities rather than initial emotional attractiveness; (4) possibilities of reuse of products or their containers, and/or recycling; and (5) the low-ecological-impact features of the manufacture, distribution, use, and disposal of products. Thus, "eco-advertising" will have to deal with the full production-use-disposal life cycle of a product, rather than focus primarily on the thrill of the moment of purchase.

6

THE COMPANY AS A LIVING SYSTEM: A FRAMEWORK FOR ORGANIZING ECOMANAGEMENT

In the remainder of this book, we shall present a detailed and coherent framework for the practice of eco-auditing. An ecological audit (as explained in Chapter 4) is an examination and review of a company's operations from the perspective of the new paradigm. The company is understood as a living system, and the theory of living systems is applied both to the conceptualization of the audit and to ecologically conscious (systemic) management. Therefore, we shall begin by reviewing a few salient features of living systems.

Systems thinking (as described in Chapter 4) involves a shift of perception from objects to relationships, from structures to processes, from building blocks to principles of organization. Living systems are integrated wholes embedded in larger wholes on which they depend. The nature of any living system derives from relationships among its component parts *and* from the relationships of the whole system to its environment.

The basic principle of organization that is characteristic of all life is the principle of self-organization (Capra 1982). This means that the order and functioning of a living system is not imposed by the environment but is established by the system itself. In other words, self-organizing systems exhibit a certain degree of autonomy. Systemically oriented managers are well aware of this fact, recognizing the company's own logic and emotionality and trying to influence the system rather than control it.

The theory of self-organizing systems distinguishes between the system's structure and its pattern of organization (Maturana and Varela 1987, 47). The pattern of organization is the totality of relationships that define the system's essential characteristics. This pattern can be described in an abstract way without referring to energy, physical substances, organisms, and so on, and without using the language of physics, chemistry, or biology. The structure of a living system is the physical realization of the pattern of organization. The same pattern may be realized in different physical and biological structures, which are described in the language of physics, chemistry, and biology.

This important distinction between structure and pattern of organization provides us with the basic conceptual tool for the eco-audit. Since the task of an eco-audit is to minimize the company's environmental impact, and since this impact concerns ecological processes involving energy, material substances, people, and other living organisms, we need to represent the company, a living system, in terms of these processes. This means that we are primarily interested in the structural aspects of the company, that is, in the physical realization of its pattern of organization.

METABOLIC FLOW AND THE ORGANIZATIONAL CHART

To represent these structural aspects in the form most suitable for an eco-audit, we designed a flow chart representing the "metabolism" of a prototypical company: the movement of materials, people, and energy from the outside, through the company, and back to the outside. Whatever its line of business—manufacturing of goods, provision of services, manipulation of information—the company will take things in, process them in various ways, and generate products and wastes. All these activities are placed visually along a metabolic flow (as illustrated in Figure 6 below), which is sufficiently general that it can be applied to companies irrespective of their central activity.

Because eco-audits are concerned with the consequences of flows of material, energy, and people; it is crucial in planning them and carrying them out to think clearly about this level of the physical realities of the company and its connections to suppliers, the community, the natural environment, and so forth. The means by which this metabolism is coordinated and managed are part of the company's pattern of organization, represented to some extent in its organizational charts, though these do not always correspond to the actual responsibilities and functions of people in a company.

If the flow chart represents the company's metabolism, its organizational chart may be seen as representing its nervous system. It is desirable to use both kinds of charts for organizing an eco-audit. Both charts together give a visual and easily grasped representation of the company. They display the full complexity of a company's structure and its relationships with its social and natural environments, so that the planning of the eco-audit will not omit critical aspects of the company's operations.

ECOMANAGING THE LIVING ORGANIZATION

Both traditional compliance auditing and more comprehensive eco-auditing make use of systematic checklists or protocols to guide investigations of a company's activities. These have evolved over the past decade-plus in a rather disorganized manner, so that a crucial aim of this book has been to give more logical rigor to the way these checklists are set up.

We have drawn upon well-developed German work, particularly that of Georg Winter, but also upon American practice; and we have extended many of these lists through our own efforts. (In assessing some technical operations, considerably more fine-grained checklists are employed.) No set of checklists can pretend to be totally

Fig. 6.

Simplified Metabolic Chart of a Prototypical Company

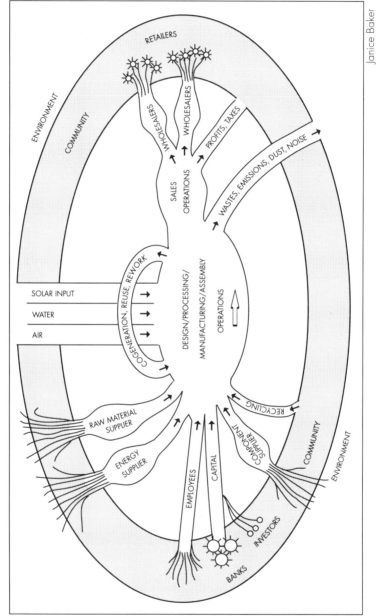

Janice Baker

exhaustive; nevertheless, we feel that use of the lists included here will ensure that no significant ecological aspects of a company's operations will be ignored. Which checklists a company chooses to focus on or do something about of course depend on factors within that particular company, and the selection will change as time goes on.

The checklists in the following chapters are organized to be used in conjunction with the metabolic flow chart (see Figure 6 above). A first group of checklists is connected with **Energy and Materials Inflows** (Chapter 7). Here we deal with energy inflows and ways they can be minimized; and with materials management, including relations with subcontractors or suppliers, whose activities often cause the bulk of a company's impact on the environment.

A second group of checklists deals with **Design, Processing, and Manufacturing Operations** (Chapter 8). The factors here are product design with "eco-friendly" criteria, including durability, sustainable use of raw materials, ethical product testing, minimal packaging waste, and so on. Here too are factors involved in manufacturing processes themselves and in recycling, both within the company and after consumer disposal of the products.

We then move on to **Sales, Marketing, Waste, and Emission Outflows** (Chapter 9). Here the checklists focus on advertising, promotion, other marketing practices, and distribution systems. Since wastes and emissions are also a form of outflow, means to identify and minimize them are included here. Some wastes, of course, can be recaptured and either reused or sold, which forms a backloop on the metabolic chart (see Figure 6).

Money, in the form of profits and investments by the company, can also be thought of as an outflow; but we have included it with a final group of checklists dealing with **Financial, Human Resource, and Other Support Structures** (Chapter 10) that underlie and affect all aspects of the metabolic flow. Methods of handling financial matters can have ecological implications; thus, they are dealt with here, along with questions of insurance. Then, we turn to workplace considerations, not only physical working conditions, such as safety, noise, and lighting, but also work organization, cafeteria nutrition, and human relations—factors that make up the "habitat" in a company.

Other supporting structures involve transportation of materials and people into and out from the company, design and management of physical plant and office facilities (including ecologically beneficial landscaping), and emergency planning. Since so much business now involves international relationships, we provide a special checklist for ecological and social criteria there.

In all these checklists—some of which are actual lists while others are in narrative form—we deal frequently with questions of implementation. We also provide, in Chapter 11, suggestions on how to set priorities in eco-auditing and how to plan a full audit. We rank priorities for action according to several scales: business considerations, ecological ones, personnel and organizational ones, and human and psychological ones. Needless to say, these different types of considerations may conflict, and difficult decisions about prioritizing may have to be resolved.

7

Energy and Materials Inflows

Checklist #1

Energy

Energy costs can decisively affect competitiveness. Looking at how energy is managed can sometimes generate new ideas for optimizing the manufacturing process.

1. Integrating an Energy Team into the Company Structure

    A. Set up a project group (consider including randomly selected staff, volunteers, or rotating appointments) with employees from production, planning, purchasing, and personnel. Make sure that employees' job descriptions include their function in this group.

B. If company is large, consider having additional energy project monitors responsible for particular areas, workplaces, workshops, or departments.

C. Arrange meetings of top management with project group and an energy specialist who can help direct discussion on given topics.

2. Becoming Informed about Energy

A. Research and gather information on relevant energy-conserving technologies or products.

B. Brainstorm alternatives; conduct employee education workshops to solicit employee suggestions.

C. Conduct a model energy audit:

- Find which departments of the company consume most electrical or heat energy, and determine costs.

- Calculate the total cost of energy purchased from non-company sources.

- Discuss what financial savings are possible and the potential effects, especially employee benefits, of the proposed reduction measures. Make financial savings clear to top management and financial departments.

- Centrally collect and review audit data on a regular basis.

D. As appropriate, solicit new ideas, formulate new objectives, and consider new technologies for reducing energy consumption.

3. Implementing Short-Term Energy Measures

A. Consider making small-scale changes in the workplace, for example, installing temperature regulators, providing extra insulation for hot water pipes, frequently cleaning surfaces of heat exchangers and air conditioner filters for maximum efficiency, and so on.

B. Install state-of-the-art monitoring equipment, when economically feasible.

C. Use heat exchangers to recover exhaust heat, and consider recirculating exhaust heat into production processes or generation of electricity.

D. Establish optimal temperatures for water used in the company in order to reduce continuous energy use.

4. Implementing Long-Term Conservation Measures

A. Check whether large amounts of energy are required for manufacture:

- Energy requirement per working hour
- Energy requirement per product unit

B. Check whether consumption, use, and maintenance by the user will involve high energy consumption or air, water, or soil pollution.

C. Check whether materials used for the product will allow it to be easily integrated into the ecological and raw materials cycles. Pay special attention to the following:

- Energy requirement for recycling (reuse)
- Energy requirement for waste disposal

D. Optimize energy-efficient design, bearing in mind all preliminary production stages and the energy required for disposal. Remember:

- Less weight saves energy
- Ceramic elements improve heat insulation

5. Communicating Progress

A. Inform employees of results in a report, and regularly in company newsletters.

B. Demonstrate energy savings achieved to interested groups both within and outside the department.

C. Inform other companies and media of successful practices.

Like reductions in electricity use, water savings translate directly (and quickly) into cost savings. One office building in Boston spent $4,720 on faucet aerators—which add air to water, so users don't turn on faucets so far. This cut water usage by 4.2 million gallons in a single year, which translated into more than $18,000 in annual water and water-heating costs. The payoff period was only three months.

CHECKLIST #2

MATERIALS

Raw material flows are vital to the global economy. Hence politics, technology, social organization, attitudes, economics, and other factors of production are all essential in developing a systemic approach to materials management. Creative input from political scientists, global thinkers, and others will be valuable for initiating a responsible policy.

The key to change lies in developing rewards for responsible suppliers and firms. Trust and loyalty between purchasing departments and subcontractors are crucial to a successful ecological program.

Since the materials eco-team will be involved in shaping innovative policies, and may require international producers to instigate large-scale change, this group needs the independence to evolve standards relevant to the company and its environment. It should also have the authority to network with other similar groups, and to direct purchasing departments to introduce its standards into contracts. To ensure compliance, this group must also be empowered to take such steps as testing sample materials in outside research labs, or sending unannounced on-site inspectors to work sites.

1. Fact-Finding

A. Collect information on raw materials used by the company and its suppliers.

- Identify basic materials requirements for present production processes and products.

- Determine points-of-origin for imported materials.

- Note any special problems of in-house use of materials, such as hazardous or environmentally damaging characteristics under various possible conditions.

- Identify other characteristics of materials, such as associated labor savings.

- Produce separate costings for water used for different purposes, and cost distribution accordingly.

- Make sure the company is in compliance with federal, state, and local laws regarding emissions, hazardous substances, and so on.

B. Collect and evaluate information from suppliers about any materials you purchase from them.

- In particular obtain details of production processes, for example:

    - Short-bath or long-bath process in the textile industry
    - Use of economical rinsing process in electroplating
    - Use of magnesium bisulfide process instead of calcium bisulfide process in paper manufacture

- Ask for details about special ecological problems arising from disposal, or remobilization into the biosphere, lithosphere, and so on.

- Collect details about pollutants during use, for example, pollutant volume and emission levels. A staff member should follow developments in legislation dealing with release of substances into air and water (see Checklist #7, Wastes and Emissions).

- Ask for information on issues such as

    - Environmental effects of alternative raw materials
    - Materials and labor savings of substitutes
    - Workplace conditions in factories, mines

- Ascertain independently the reliability of information from suppliers, and check their business policy and economic status, the efficiency of transportation, and so on.

C. Solicit and catalog ideas from industries, nonprofit environmental institutes, research laboratories, ecology journals, and, where appropriate, from company engineering, research, and development departments.

D. Centralize information on alternative products, raw materials substitutions, and new technologies; make this information accessible to all employees, even those not involved in the materials eco-team.

E. At regular meetings, brainstorm ideal and contractual standards for basic environmental and social goals. The participation of outside consultants is strongly recommended.

2. Adopting Ecological Strategies and Practices

A. Improve on-site storage of raw materials.

- Label and restrict access to all hazardous substances.

- Apply ecological principles in designing and maintaining storage facilities, for example:
  - Low-exhaust forklift trucks
  - Reusable containers

B. Install advanced equipment.

- Use modern painting equipment.

C. Improve efficiency.

- Use catalysts and converters to improve yield from raw materials or reduce emissions.

- Use minimal amounts of cooling water.

- Install state-of-the-art automatic measuring and control technology.

- To monitor water use, install thermometers, expansion valves, and flow reducers.

- Substitute rainwater rather than groundwater, if possible.

D. Recover/Recycle.

- Always recover heavy metals, acids, and organic solvents.

- Devise techniques to facilitate raw materials recovery (for example, do not mix substances; in wet processes, reduce rinsing and cleaning water).

- Recycle rinsing and cleaning water.

- Recycle, recirculate, or reuse useful substances in effluent or convert them into other useful products.

- Separate and reprocess industrial sewage water.

- Use grey water for toilet flushing.

> As high-quality water becomes scarcer, cutting water use in industrial processes will have increased payoffs. By recirculating water, Gillette cut its use of water in razor-blade manufacturing from 730 million to 156 million gallons a year—saving about $1.5 million in yearly water and sewage costs.

E. Replace hazardous materials with less hazardous ones.

- Replace cadmium coatings with zinc.

- Use low- rather than high-sulfur coal.

- Replace asbestos in brake and coupling linings.

- Replace chlorinated hydrocarbons in cold cleaning solvent.

- Replace PCB transformers.

F. Increase efficiency of international, national, and intercompany transportation.

- Optimize routes and shipment schedules to avoid waste of resources.

■ Favor transportation methods that have reduced environmental costs.

3. Managing Component Parts

A. Conduct components inventory.

■ Catalog product components for all manufactured products, and, as far as is compatible with trade secrets, for supplied products.

■ Check whether components can be recycled:

■ Transformers containing PCBs need special disposal

■ Fluorescent lamps contain dangerous metals and should be carefully returned to the manufacturer

4. Negotiating with Suppliers

A. Specify new ecological and workplace standards in contracts with suppliers and subcontractors; communicate to them your corporate strategy or mission.

B. In negotiating contracts, detail exceptional circumstances, such as political repression or flagrant national disregard for human rights, which would make a region or nation unacceptable for your business.

C. Favor suppliers and subcontractors who meet your new standards and timetables, and show willingness to negotiate about longer-term goals.

Compact fluorescent bulbs last about 10,000 hours (compared with the 750 hours of a standard bulb) and use about a quarter as much electricity for the light produced. Since bulb-changing is infrequent, significant labor costs are saved, in addition to massive energy costs. If local suppliers cannot provide you with bulbs and information, contact the "Green Lights" program in the Global Change Division of EPA, 401 M Street, SW, Washington, DC 20460. Telephone: (202) 382-4992.

5. Implementing More Ecologically Advanced Strategies and Practices

A. Stimulate markets for new sustainable technologies and less environmentally damaging production processes.

- In mining, for example, favor suppliers who have integrated processes of wastewater reclamation, erosion control, habitat restoration.

- In agriculture, favor suppliers who practice biocontrol, use minimal or no artificial fertilizers or pesticides, and so forth.

- Favor suppliers who use alternative fuels, energy, or transportation that is less environmentally damaging.

- Encourage technologies and processes that foster ecological innovation and long-term sustainability.

B. Independently verify whether contract goals are being met by subcontractors.

- Consider requiring bills-of-lading, certifications (if points-of-origin may be obscure), clearance certificates, quality analyses results.

- Involve own engineering or research and development departments as well as independent labs to analyze dangerous materials and contaminants and to assess alternatives.

C. Form cooperative buying groups with similar companies in order to stimulate markets for environmentally responsible production.

8

DESIGN, PROCESSING, AND MANUFACTURING OPERATIONS

CHECKLIST #3

PRODUCT DESIGN AND DEVELOPMENT

For long-term environmental changes to occur, ecological thinking must be introduced into the design and development stages of production. If the firm is large enough to have managers for each product line, give them a significant share of responsibility for the environmental impact of their product.

Innovative product design can be enhanced by looking at the larger service or process goal that a product addresses. For example, when AT&T redefined themselves not as a telephone company but as being in the business of communication, a myriad of product and service options opened up, from voicemail to video. Volkswagen sees itself as in the business of transportation, not exclusively as a car company. Looking at the process rather than the product can broaden the conceptual framework for product development and generate new ideas for serving the customer, while making it easier to change or let go of specific, ecologically unsound products.

Keep a special eye on developing new products from current manufacturing by-products. This can eliminate waste and create products at tremendous cost savings on both the raw material and waste disposal sides (see Checklist #4, Manufacturing and Production).

1. Catalog Current Products to Determine Which Could Be Improved by Eco-Friendly Design

A. Integrate ecological thinking into the evaluation of the full cycle of product conception, specification, production, use, reuse, and ultimate disposition.

B. Research possible new uses for obsolescent products.

C. Make new products adaptable to foreseeable improvements in science and technology.

D. Design parts to have multiple uses and to be useable in different products. To this end, aim for standardization of parts used.

   ■ Make use of ASA/DIN standards.

E. Provide room for additional components by avoiding integrated construction.

F. Make technical provision for enlargement of product capacity, include

   ■ Capacity reserves
   ■ Multiple connectors

2. Design Products for Effective Maintenance and Durability

A. Increase the functional life of products.

B. Store unfinished products so that wear and tear are minimized.

C. Design products to facilitate repair and the recycling of component parts.

D. Avoid frequent design changes for stylistic and marketing purposes; make classic, durable design your trademark.

E. Especially avoid "disposable" products.

F. Seek ways to limit the energy required to use, maintain, and repair products.

3. Make Sustainable, Ethical Use of Raw Materials in Design

A. Favor use of materials derived from sustainable systems of production (or from recycled products). Place a high priority on designing products that use raw materials that are by-products from the company's existing production processes.

B. To facilitate recycling, consider whether constituent raw materials can be reused or recycled, and how much energy is required for this process.

C. Avoid combining materials that are incompatible for future reuse or recycling.

- Avoid using aluminum cans with steel tops.

- Carefully select printing inks and dyes when using them on products destined for recycling.

D. Use fewer raw materials per product.

4. Product Testing

A. Establish guidelines for dealing with the issue of animal experimentation.

- Substitute computer modeling or cell culture for whole animal studies.

- If whole animal testing is essential, provide stringent guidelines for humane treatment of test subjects (e.g., press for alternatives to "sacrifice" of test individuals).

- Take an absolute position against testing on animals taken from the wild and of course on endangered or threatened species.

B. For aerodynamic products, use computer simulation or experiments to facilitate efficient design.

C. Test products for the diversity of consumers who will use them, even if in smaller numbers.

- Test for differences between men and women. (Catheters for heart attacks, for example, have been sized for men's bodies.)

- Test for differences between cultural groups. (Genetic differences or predispositions, dietary constraints, social taboos, and religious restrictions are among the issues that can impact on appropriate product use. This is particularly true for internationally marketed products.)

- Test for differences between socioeconomic groups, job categories, and education levels. (Working night shifts and swing shifts, working double shifts or doing extremely hard physical labor, level of literacy, and access to technology, such as refrigeration, telecommunications, and efficient transportation, are among the factors that can influence appropriate product use and effectiveness.)

- Test for differences in sexual orientation, life-style, and physical abilities.

A good source of ongoing information: *The Green Business Letter,* 1526 Connecticut Avenue, NW, Washington, DC 20036. Telephone: (800) 955-GREEN.

---

5. During Design Phase, Aim to Reduce or Eliminate Toxic Materials in Both Products and Production Processes

A. Find suitable substitutes for hazardous dyes and preservatives on paper, cloth, wood, and so on.

6. Design for Consumer Health and Well-Being

A. Consider health of customers during design.

- Design apparel that complements the biological needs of the human body.

- Minimize or eliminate harmful preservatives, fats, trace contaminants, and so forth in food products.

B. Make products easy to use; include clear instructions to minimize risk of accidents and injury, and to prevent stress.

- Make machines as self-explanatory as possible.
- Use icon markings for control knobs.
- Incorporate health warnings into the design of the product itself, on the side of a machine, on hangtags, on containers.

C. Make provisions for those who fall outside the scope of normal marketing stereotypes in terms of weight, physical ability, linguistic fluency, literacy, and so forth.

7. Design to Reduce Social, Cultural, and Economic Inequality

A. It is unethical to reinforce stereotypes based on race, ethnicity, gender, and sexual orientation in designing and selling products.

B. Do not make high cost and inaccessibility the selling point of products.

8. Respect Life Forms and Ecosystems

A. Avoid using products or parts of animals taken from the wild, especially endangered or threatened species.

B. Consider alternatives for the use of animal parts as raw materials.

C. With regard to plants, avoid supporting exploitation of endangered and threatened plant species, or deforestation/defoliation that endangers bioregions.

D. Consider introducing a high-prestige line of products that represents the culmination of advanced ecological thinking.

E. Consider using ecological and preservation themes in fabric patterns, decorative designs on products, and so on.

9. Avoid Wasteful Packaging

A. Establish whether suppliers are able to use minimal returnable/recyclable/organically degradable packaging.

B. Use standardized packaging in order to make optimum use of transport and storage space.

C. Select the packaging material with the lowest energy input requirements.

D. Design packaging to be reusable, either as packaging or for other purposes.

E. Collect paper and cardboard for recycling.

F. Minimize use of plastics, styrofoam; consider popcorn and other biodegradable or recyclable materials.

G. Consider eliminating all packaging by a set date. Consider a policy to refuse materials received from suppliers who don't eliminate packaging.

CHECKLIST #4

MANUFACTURING AND PRODUCTION

1. Establish a Fact-Finding and Research Group

A. Analyze existing manufacturing processes and technologies.

B. Propose ecologically favorable alternatives in the short term.

C. Keep informed about relevant innovations (emerging technologies, new processes, and products) that would improve the company's ecological and social performance over the long run, even if expensive in the short term.

D. Make certain that company is complying with, or exceeding, existing environmental protection standards.

2. Improve the Ecological Performance of Existing Systems and Materials in the Short Term

A. Introduce additives and catalysts that will improve raw materials yield and/or reduce harmful emissions in manufacturing.

B. Increase energy efficiency by insulating, sealing, or otherwise protecting equipment and materials to be used at high or low temperatures.

C. Check and repair all leaks in existing equipment used for circulating or storing gases and liquids (e.g., valves, pumps, pipes, shut-off devices).

D. Regularly check pollutant treatment equipment for proper operation and efficiency.

E. Reduce noise by isolating machinery, insulating, and other means. (Provide employees with comfortable ear protection against noise.)

F. Reduce vibrations generated by equipment.

G. Make employee safety a priority.

- Provide basic employee training in first aid, workplace hazards, and so forth.

- Conveniently locate first aid equipment and stations (e.g., eyewashes, showers).

- Monitor employee health complaints for early indication of hazardous and toxic contact.

- On a voluntary basis, have blood and urine samples analyzed for employee uptake of hazardous and toxic chemicals.

3. Continuously Upgrade and Redesign Production for Long-Term Benefits

A. Replace hazardous chemicals with ones that pose fewer human health hazards and/or cause less pollution (see also Checklist #2, Materials). This will significantly benefit employees and the community.

- Find substitutes for known carcinogens and other major hazards.

- Do not store/use explosives or corrosives near toxics, which could create a costly environmental accident.

B. Upgrade with technologies that improve company's ecological and human health record (see also Checklist #7, Wastes and Emissions).

- Favor technologies that give improved input and output ratio.

- Choose more reliable automatic measuring and control technologies.

- Install automatic monitors and warning systems for emergencies.

C. Aim to improve postproduction, or "end-of-pipe," environmental protection equipment.

- Install sophisticated "scrubbers" for reducing hazardous emissions from air stacks.

- Adopt "Best Available Technology" as a standard.

D. Replace inefficient and highly polluting energy systems with efficient ones that are less damaging to the environment.

- Use alternative sources such as solar and wind; investigate photovoltaics.

- Design systems to reuse process waste heat; consider co-generation (see also Checklist #1, Energy).

E. Avoid intermediate storage by switching from discontinuous manufacture to continuous processes.

F. Adopt hermetic processes especially for dangerous dust-producing substances, such as asbestos and fiberglass.

4. Recover, Recycle, and Reprocess

A. Recycle or reuse effluents that contain useful substances (see also Checklist #5, Recycling).

B. Responsibly recycle, reprocess, recover or, if necessary, dispose of wastes that contain harmful substances.

5. Responsible Manufacturing

A. Redesign manufacturing processes to eliminate unwanted substances from the production stream.

B. If a product is found to be manufactured or produced in an unsafe manner given current specifications, then redesign the product and/or production process.

C. If a product cannot be manufactured or produced in a safe manner under current specifications, then eliminate—or find suitable alternatives for—the product and/or its production process.

CHECKLIST #5

RECYCLING

Recycling is a popular, labor-intensive strategy to mitigate some effects of raw materials exploitation. To be effective, strong markets for recycled components and finished goods must be stimulated. Ecologically conscious firms should therefore not only support these markets but also inquire whether or not materials designated for recycling are actually being reprocessed and for what products. Political influence should be used to promote government backing for use of recycled products.

1. Fact-Finding

A. Set up a recycling management team—with representatives from product design, materials, purchasing and marketing, and independent specialists—to oversee and evaluate all recycling and use of recycled products. Ensure that the team is empowered to make necessary changes.

B. Note departments of the corporation that consume products that can be replaced by recycled products.

- Weigh costs of switching to the alternatives against the estimated environmental benefits; consider relative "visibility" of changes.

- Assess regional or large-scale environmental impact of particular recycling operations, and develop guidelines for deciding when recycling is appropriate.

- Consider especially the energy, labor, and capital requirements of recycling versus any pollutant effects of current disposal arrangements. Analyze consumer demand for the recycled product.

- Weigh the practical costs of recycling against estimated environmental benefit.

C. Ensure that recycled products are not hazardous to those who produce or use them; for example, favor recycled paper that is free of dioxin.

2. Recycling in Production Facilities, Offices, Retail Outlets, and Similar Locations

A. It is preferable that product design facilitate recycling (see also Checklist #3, Product Design and Development).

- Use fewer or more easily separable raw materials.
- Standardize components.
- Avoid nonbiodegradable materials.

B. Change mix of products or services, organizational structures, transportation or communication systems, and so on, to optimize recycling.

C. Recover raw materials and reduce waste in the production process.

- Using materials and components inventories, note any possibilities for recycling waste produce into own or external production.

D. Conveniently place and label recycling bins for selected materials.

E. Provide opportunities for employees to bring materials from home for recycling if they have no other alternative.

F. Bring in an outside contractor to facilitate recycling.

G. Within the company, substitute computer "e-mail" for typed paper memos and communications.

H. Educate customers (using product labels or hangtags) to emphasize recyclable components of products.

I. Offer customer rebates for recycling your products (e.g., for returning worn cotton goods to become cotton rag paper).

3. Negotiating with Recycling Firms

A. Research and select firms that meet criteria determined by recycling management team, seem willing to negotiate, and are not owned by corporations with a history of mistreating the environment or employees.

B. To reduce costs, consider purchasing directly from firms that produce goods from recycled materials.

C. If possible, purchase recycled products from the same companies that recycle your waste.

D. Should suppliers of materials and components be in a good position to recycle associated by-products, incorporate recycling requirements into contracts.

E. Negotiate optimal transport routes with recycling firms and other companies that recycle.

F. Make sure that the recycling firm is responsibly handling materials.

4. Implementing More Ecologically Advanced Strategies and Principles

A. Aim to stimulate the market for recycled products by informative advertising, displays in retail outlets, and product labels.

B. Form computer information networks with other corporations about suppliers and recyclers, to facilitate flow of reusable and recycled materials.

C. Form computer information networks with other corporations about responsible recyclers and suppliers of recycled goods.

D. Progressively change product and package design in ways that make recycling easier (see also Checklist #2, Materials, and Ckecklist #3, Product Design and Development).

E. Increasingly try to use biodegradable substances in all your processes.

F. Find ways to recycle waste produced by the company into other products. Create your own closed-loop system.

New German Recycling Law

A sweeping new German recycling law went into effect April 1, 1992, requiring all businesses to collect and recycle the packaging they use for their products. By January 1993, 50 percent of all consumer products packaging will have to be recycled; and by 1995, 80 percent must be recycled.

Although companies originally claimed that the law would be unworkable, 600 firms eventually banded together to form Duales System Deutschland, a corporation that assists local governments in collecting materials and recycling them. Duales System has distributed large yellow recycling bins to half the German population—40 million people— and hopes to reach 90 percent of the population by the end of the year.

Packagers pay Duales System a fee ranging from one cent to $2 per product. In return, their product is marked with a distinctive green dot, and its packaging is collected and recycled in the Duales System program.

Environmentalists fault the German law for placing too much emphasis on recycling instead of promoting reusable packaging or waste reduction. The system has also created an urgent need for more sorting and recycling plants, which are slowly being built. Despite these problems, how-ever, the German law has rapidly produced one of the most ambitious and exciting national recycling programs in the world.

9

SALES, MARKETING, WASTE, AND EMISSION OUTFLOWS

CHECKLIST #6

MARKETING AND SALES

Marketing is comprised of the aggregate steps involved in getting your product to consumers. This includes how you promote, price, and distribute your products.

1. Set Up Teams To Evaluate and Reconsider Current Marketing

2. Promotion

  A. Package Design (see also Checklist #3, Product Design and Development)
- Evaluate and reconsider current designs.

- In conjunction with the materials team, devise sensible packaging made from environmentally acceptable materials.

- Avoid overpackaging (i.e., using unnecessarily large containers or double wrapping).

- Consider developing packages that travel well but use minimal materials.

- Use "eco-seals" on your packaging to highlight your product's environmentally positive features (see Callenbach 1990).

B. Sales

- Evaluate and reconsider current style.

- Provide information to your customer on the ecological benefits of your products.

- Provide post-sales and advisory services to ensure that the product is used and disposed of in an acceptable manner.

- If higher prices cannot be avoided as a result of ecologically sound manufacturing processes, make it clear to distributors and consumers how the costs are calculated (discuss price differentials based on ecological factors).

- If you work through retailers, consider providing an 800 number (in the United States) to answer the final customer questions about the ecological effects of your product.

C. Retailing

- Evaluate and reconsider current arrangements.

- Negotiate with your retailers to present your product in a manner that is in accordance with your ecological marketing strategy.

- If you feel your retailers are not in accord with the image you wish to promote, consider opening your own stores where you have more control over your company image and the presentation of your products, and where you can more easily monitor consumer preferences.

D. Advertising

- Evaluate and reconsider current media and levels of effort.

- Avoid use of advertising media that is not ecological (i.e., coated papers and toxic inks).

- Use "eco-seals" in your advertisements to emphasize the eco-friendly features of your product.

- If you use direct mail, avoid duplication in mailings; consider targeting different catalogs to different audiences.

3. Distribution

A. Evaluate and reconsider existing systems.

- Give preference to existing transport systems that have reduced environmental costs in terms of energy consumption and pollution.

- Research and support the development of more ecologically sound transportation systems.

4. Establish and Implement Strategy (based on above considerations)

A. Determine and target customer sectors most likely to be affected by advertising that stresses ecological factors.

B. Prioritize products or product categories to promote in an ecological campaign.

C. Periodically monitor the success of the above strategies in economic terms and revise if necessary.

D. Work with the public relations group to monitor the company's profile with respect to these decisions, and revise strategy if necessary.

E. Provide monetary bonuses or other incentives for achieving or surpassing targets.

F. Consider implementing (and publicizing) marketing or sales strategies that directly benefit environmentally or socially significant programs and/or projects.

- Designate a percentage of total company sales or profits for this purpose.
- Designate a portion of profits from a specific product line for this purpose.
- Consider including local and regional, as well as international projects in this category.

CHECKLIST #7

WASTES AND EMISSIONS

Every part of a company creates pollution of some kind. Often, the various divisions produce very different types of pollution. Thus, you may find it useful to divide your teams into such categories as research and development, manufacturing, and office.

1. Set Up Teams to Evaluate
- Waste production and disposal
- Emissions and emission controls

A. Consider including both employees and representatives from other companies with specific technical knowledge of the processes producing waste and emissions, disposal arrangements, and emission controls.

B. Randomly select several team members from your employees to encourage creative solutions.

C. Consider asking representatives from your suppliers, from other companies in your industry, and from your disposal companies to join your effort.

D. Select several people well versed in legal and technical matters who would be able to knowledgeably investigate existing environmental laws with respect to emission controls, noise, toxic waste, water pollution, and so forth.

2. Identify Waste Products and Current Means of Disposal

A. Specify the individual by-products (e.g., wood, paper, chemical compounds, asbestos).

B. Note the origins of these by-products (production process, office waste, development waste), specifically indicating the process by which the waste is produced (i.e., the actual chemical and physical processes).

C. Identify and rank the toxicity, lifetime, and general disposal problems of all waste (noting medical hazards to workers, land and water pollution, special disposal conditions for the item to biodegrade, and so on).

D. Evaluate existing disposal arrangements, noting their effectiveness given the above ranking and their compliance with current laws.

Ben and Jerry's Homemade Ice Cream has developed a complete environmental program affecting every aspect of the company. One particular achievement is that they now sell more than a thousand plastic pails per week to a recycler; this costs $6,500 a year, where landfill disposal formerly cost $30,000. (The company would have preferred to reuse the pails, but health regulations forbid this.)

---

3. Identify Emissions and Current Emissions Levels

A. Itemize all emissions emanating from your factories or buildings (including noise, gases, particulates, odors).

B. Indicate the origins of these emissions, noting the specific processes that produce the emissions.

C. Identify and rank the medical and ecological consequences of each emission.

D. Note emissions controls currently in place for each discharge, indicating inadequacies and degree of compliance with current laws.

E. Prioritize current emissions and control measures that must be changed.

4. Investigate Alternatives for Reducing or Eliminating Waste and Emissions

(Note: consider getting help or referrals from sources such as the Environmental Protection Agency.)

A. Use your two lists of priorities as a starting point for this investigation.

B. Seek other production methods whereby the creation of emissions and waste could be avoided altogether.

C. Seek alternative methods that would reduce their production.

D. Consider physical or chemical processes that would render the waste harmless (i.e., a mixture of methyl alcohol, formic acid, acetic acid, and ester heated to 900–1000 degrees Celsius will form carbon dioxide and water).

E. Consider whether any waste products could be used as raw materials for another production process within the company or could be sold to another company (in office situations, paper can be shredded and reused for packing materials or note pads).

F. Research more appropriate disposal methods (i.e., those with a higher degree of safety, or those that would more readily cause the waste to biodegrade).

G. Rank each alternative in terms of its results, ease of implementation, and financial cost (paying particular attention to the possibility that a new method may decrease noxious emissions while yielding another harmful by-product).

H. Select alternatives to pursue immediately (those which are most urgent from your above lists of priorities, followed by those producing the most results or costing the least).

5. Design a Strategy and Set Up Infrastructure to Support It

A. Devise an action plan (note steps to be taken, make a deadline, assign a task force and review committee who will ensure that environmental objectives are continually met).

B. For the long term, assign an experienced staff member or consultant to continually inform your decision makers of laws and regulations pertaining to environmental protection (make sure he or she provides you periodically with written reports).

C. Attend to all waste management systems.

- Provide conveniently located receptacles for storing by-products.

- Install collection points for used oil, solvents, solutions, acids, dyes, and so on.

- Store toxic waste in well-ventilated areas away from employees and heat.

D. Provide office containers for waste paper, plastics, glass, aluminum, and metals, such as staples, paper clips, and bottle caps (see also Checklist #5, Recycling).

E. If you have your own retail store, establish recycling centers for your customers.

F. If you are the distributor, set up recycling channels for your customers.

6. Negotiate with Your Suppliers and Disposal Firms

A. Have suppliers arrange for pick up of waste associated with their product (i.e., suppliers pick up waste that they can reuse, or they contract with a local recycling company).

B. In contracts with suppliers, add a clause requiring them to provide full information on product characteristics and materials (thus, the supplier is liable for any misinformation).

C. Make spot checks to ensure that disposal conditions are adequate (perhaps even form an organization with other clients that would monitor the disposal process).

10

FINANCIAL, HUMAN RESOURCE, AND OTHER SUPPORT STRUCTURES

CHECKLIST #8

FINANCE

As governments increasingly seek to shape corporate choices to minimize ecological damage, a great variety of financial implications are emerging. Thus, tax write-offs are sometimes given for the adoption of emission-minimizing equipment; utility rates (and hence profits) are allowed to rise to finance energy-conservation measures; procurement policies are designed to favor ecologically desirable products such as recycled paper; the location of new or expanded facilities is subject to increasingly stringent environmental impact reports. Hence, investment strategies must more and more be framed in terms of the ecological context.

In England and Germany, some government grants are available for certain kinds of environmental protection research or improvements. The German government offers various important tax advantages and low-interest loans. In the United States, industrial waste-water treatment may be eligible for federal grants; some loans and grants are also available from state sources. The European Development Bank in Luxembourg offers loans for investment in environmental protection, often on better terms than those of national banks. The Commission of the European Communities in Brussels offers funds for demonstration or model projects.

All investments should routinely be subjected to ecological evaluation. Ask, for example:

- Will it increase pollution?

- Will it increase ecological risks?

- Will it protect the environment?

- Will it protect the environment and also increase profitability?

The phasing of new investment can be ecologically sensitive. If a new lower-pollution technology is in the offing, it may be reasonable, regulations permitting, to delay replacement or fixes of the current generation of equipment. Sometimes accelerated replacement of polluting equipment may be desirable.

If a particular investment is likely to cause or increase pollution, the financial dimensions of the costs and risks involved must be considered. The following are special factors that can be costly to ignore:

- Probable future costs for disposal of wastes

- Possible changes in regulatory thresholds

- Possible income from developing sales of by-products that would be pollutants if released

The "parking" of company funds can have ecological implications. Consider whether using banks within the company's bioregion will help keep capital local and thus foster local community strength, including environmentally desirable investments.

Evaluate whether employee 401(k) or other corporate pension plans include environmentally and socially responsible investment options.

Traditional investment costing methods usually discriminate against long-term projects, which bear most of their fruit in later years. So-called "dynamic" costing methods, that is, the capital value method and the internal interest method, may be preferable.

Investing solely in end-of-the-pipe measures is generally far more expensive in terms of results than making more systemic changes. Paying attention to only one troublesome aspect of a production process at a time, rather than the whole, is also generally needlessly costly.

The buying or selling of emissions allowances, while controversial among environmentalists, can have very large investment consequences. Specialists in "environmental property auditing" investigate potential ecological risks in the buying and selling of real property and corporations.

Insurance against massive ecological risks is being explored, sometimes through government, as with oil spills; it already exists for nuclear accidents (though on an extremely limited scale considering potential damages). In most European countries, national health services and other measures provide a certain basic "insurance" for employees and citizens. In special-risk industries, such as mining and chemicals, companies sometimes provide accident and life insurance.

While normal liability insurance offers a good deal of protection for most business risks, the liability consequences of some industrial processes, as has been demonstrated by asbestos, can be immense and are seldom insurable; companies and their executives persist in them knowingly at great peril. Since the law is evolving rapidly in this area, a company using risky technologies must make it a high priority to keep abreast of developments.

Facilities insurance should be reviewed to ascertain its coverage of ecologically related damage. Insurance also exists to cover interruption of production from such ecological causes as toxic spills.

CHECKLIST #9

INVESTMENTS

1. Establish an Eco-Investment Strategy

A. Determine ecological criteria you wish to follow in your investments.

- Rank these criteria in terms of urgency to environment and society.

- Target your investments toward companies and governmental and nongovernmental agencies that follow your ranking.

2. Make the Investments

A. Seek out investment institutions whose investment philosophies support your ecological criteria.

B. Use your "investor power" to move your own financial institution toward considering adopting more ecological investment principles.

- Think about purchasing local, state, or federal bonds supporting ecologically sound investment measures.

- Research potential eco-friendly investments (e.g., companies that need financing to make ecological improvements).

C. Justify your ecological investments to your stockholders.

D. Invest in your employees: provide incentive stock purchase plans and compensation benefits to reward improved ecological performance on all levels within the company.

3. Lobby for Eco-Investment Incentives

A. Organize a group to lobby for tax credits for specific environmental investments made by companies.

B. Support government or private aid for environmental improvements.

4. Support Community Organizations

A. Offer grants for organizations, local groups, and institutions involved in ecological or human-services projects.

CHECKLIST #10

THE WORKPLACE

WORKING CONDITIONS

The internal environment of a company is of critical importance to the physical and mental health of everyone who works there, and hence to the overall welfare of the company. Indeed, since people in the company spend a large proportion of their waking hours in the company "habitat," working conditions there may be thought of as an important "product" that is consumed by these people, along with the products that are sold to customers outside the company. Working conditions include many factors besides those narrowly connected with work tasks.

Moreover, if stressful conditions of bad lighting or ventilation, noise, dust, toxics, or physical danger are not avoided, employees can hardly be asked to take a creative interest in general environmental matters. The same holds true if workers face poor social conditions, such as no job security, poor supervision, limited opportunities for promotion or learning, discrimination, or punitive motivation systems. Internal and external environmental concerns are thus tightly linked, and need to be treated with an integrated approach.

Noise, including Low-Frequency Vibration

Noise from machinery can often be reduced, through cushioning or springs, shielding, sound-absorbent enclosures, venting to the outside, and so on. Noise from subsidiary activities can also be severe and must be considered. Intermittent noises may be especially irritating and distracting. In general, noise can be contained by interposing continuous mass (no cracks or holes) between source and hearers, for example, heavy plate glass, metal, or concrete. Structural isolation may sometimes be needed to prevent transmission of sound. Persons exposed to loud noise should use personal protective muffling equipment, and need regular medical check-ups.

Lighting and Colors

Minimum lighting intensities for different tasks are often prescribed by regulations. Many other factors affect employee comfort and performance, however, some of which may also be subject to regulations: contrast ratios between light and dark areas, reflectance of surfaces, direction of light sources, and so forth. (For example, computer terminals require relatively low-level and indirect lighting.) Since employees are the best judges of their own lighting needs, they should be given considerable latitude in choosing and arranging light sources.

Fluorescent lamps, which are environmentally attractive because of their high energy efficiency, pose some special problems. Combining tubes of different light colors is desirable to approximate full-spectrum sunlight, which is most comfortable for people; specially made tubes also achieve this, as do some bulb-shaped lamps. Flickering can be avoided by replacing worn-out ballasts, or using electronic devices or three-phase switching.

Colors in a work environment can have strong effects, but there is great debate over particular color effects—some "reds" are more restful than some "greens," for instance. It is generally felt that a light-colored ceiling seems higher than the same ceiling painted a dark color. A skillful decorator, in consultation with employees, will apply many such rules of thumb to producing a comfortable environment.

Electromagnetic Fields

Recent research has indicated that people (especially children and pregnant women) are affected by relatively low-level magnetic and electric fields, which are generated by much modern machinery (as well as by such devices as electric blankets) and pass through ordinary walls and floors. International attitudes vary in caution, with some researchers holding that danger levels are very low or nonexistent. Nevertheless, the level of concern among scientists has been rising steadily, leading to an array of considerations.

Video display terminals, for example, produce strong electromagnetic fields to the sides and rear especially, and should not be grouped closely or in large numbers. Women who are newly pregnant or about to become pregnant should not work with them. Spaces near transformers or other equipment or wires carrying large electrical currents, whether inside or outside of buildings, are not good places for people to spend large amounts of time. Facilities with human occupants should not be located under or near high-voltage transmission lines.

"Climate"

From the point of view of people's comfort, quiet natural ventilation is preferable to closed forced-air ventilation systems for much of the year in many climates. Architects are learning how to use solar energy, natural wind input, buildings' capacities for heat retention and exclusion, and similar advanced techniques, to produce structures whose energy consumption is modest even under quite severe conditions.

Where closed systems are employed, particular attention is required for humidity, variations in air speed with respect to vents, drafts, temperature gradients between head and foot levels, and so forth. Radiative heat from warm surfaces can be a cause of discomfort, requiring attention. If heat generated by lamps, equipment, and human bodies cannot be dissipated through natural ventilation, solar-driven air-conditioning equipment can be considered.

Hazardous Substances

See Checklist #7, Wastes and Emissions.

Equipment

A large number of considerations bear on equipment design; thus, we can only suggest a sampling here. The principle of one-function, one-switch should be followed to minimize operator errors;

emergency "off" switches should be clearly marked and easily accessible. Ergonomic design of all equipment should be the rule, to minimize fatigue. Equipment and work tasks should be designed to provide frequent interruptions of repetitive movements and to minimize physiological hazards. Asymmetrical and excessive muscular exertion are to be avoided. Balance and variety are desirable between "private" areas on machines and those that are shared for tasks on which people cooperate.

Safety

Many work environments are inherently dangerous, and yet safety precautions easily become part of the ignored "background." An audit can bring them to everybody's attention again. Danger signs and symbols (including color coding) should be reviewed. Protective devices and equipment may need to be installed or repaired; in some cases, workers under production pressure may have disabled safety devices— a sign that they require redesign so as not to inhibit production. Anti-dazzle and anti-spatter devices must be reviewed. Traffic routes should be defined and clearly marked to eliminate collisions of moving equipment and people. The wearing of necessary protective clothing or other personal equipment must be ensured.

Areas around automatic machinery require particular attention; safety barriers or fences are needed to prevent people from entering dangerous areas. If machinery can throw waste or parts, possible trajectories must be guarded. Take particular pains with safety during periods of installation or maintenance, when normal safety equipment is dismantled or not yet in place.

Work Organization

The apparent advantages of a rigid assembly-line division of labor are often undercut by its human disadvantages: high absentee and error rates, employee dissatisfaction and rapid turnover. Developing a satisfactory internal environment is therefore inevitably concerned with the description and content of jobs. While every company's needs and possibilities are different, and employee "cultures" vary from community to community, certain principles are widely believed to help provide a healthy working environment:

Job Design

- Organize operations to include teamwork; groups that have some degree of authority over how they collectively do their work are generally more efficient, creative, and contented.

- Design jobs to prevent the stress of excessive repetition, rigid timing, social isolation, physical strength, and precision of movement.

- Provide regular, on-the-job learning experiences for employees at all levels. Recognize that mistakes are part of the learning process.

Stake in Organizational Performance

- Create opportunities for participation in decision making.

- Link responsibility for a task with the authority required to carry it out.

- Share rewards from productivity improvements. This can include profit sharing, employee ownership, recognition, promotion, pay, and other benefits.

Motivation

- Motivate employees positively, not punitively. Assure that individuals are rewarded for a job well done and receive concrete, constructive feedback and training, if appropriate, in areas that need improvement.

- Provide means for employees to responsibly balance work and family life, including flexible work times.

- Work toward diversity within and reduce distinctions between all levels of the organization by compensation, culture, gender, sexual orientation, and so forth.

Basic Rights

- Provide fair pay, benefits, and job security.

- Guarantee the right to free speech and access to information.

- Enable employees to raise concerns with those in authority and guarantee due process for those who feel unfairly treated.

Food

Meals eaten in company cafeterias often make up a major part of employees' diets, and are therefore important for the maintenance of health and productivity. Healthy eating patterns at work may carry over to home dietary practices. Moreover, a company's expenses for health insurance, as well as losses through medical absences, can be reduced by improving the employees' overall health.

A company is wise to provide a wide range of nutritional and health information to all employees. Basic and well-established facts about the bad effects of diets high in fat, salt, and sugar should be made available through booklets, bulletin-board materials, and after-hours lectures to which spouses, domestic partners, and friends are invited. Some companies provide gyms or other exercise facilities (and conduct classes to augment individual alcohol and weight-reduction programs). Others provide shower and changing rooms so that some employees can obtain desirable exercise by bicycling to work.

If an outside food concessionaire runs the company cafeteria, its menus should be nutritionally audited; if the concessionaire is unable or unwilling to make needed improvements, the company should consider operating its own kitchen. Having a kitchen on the premises generally provides fresher and more nutritious meals, better matched to the tastes of the employees. Edible wastes, if they cannot be avoided, can sometimes be donated to nonprofit food kitchens. The surroundings in the cafeteria should be pleasant, with natural light, ventilation, and greenery. Plastic and "disposable" plates, cups, and utensils should be avoided or carefully recycled. Inedible food wastes should be composted for use on company landscaping.

People's feelings about food habits run deep, so improving the healthiness of cafeteria food (while preserving or encouraging ethnic as well as international tastes) needs to be accomplished by gentle stages. Nevertheless, it should include such basic goals as:

- Lower fat, salt, and sugar content
- More fiber content
- More (fresh) vegetables and fruits

It can be helpful to label cafeteria dishes and foods with protein, sodium, calories, and fat content as well as prices. Menus should provide sufficient alternatives for vegetarian employees. When breakfast is offered, it should include low-fat yogurt, oatmeal, whole-wheat rolls, and other alternatives to the "standard" high-cholesterol breakfast. Teas, including noncaffeinated or herb teas, should always be available.

Vending machines inside or around company facilities should also be reviewed, to make sure they offer fruit juices and low- or nonfat milk as an alternative to soda drinks and coffee; and nuts, sunflower seeds, and healthy snack bars as alternatives to candy bars and chips. If concessionaires are unable to provide these, the company should operate its own machines.

Household Counseling

While industry is the greatest single source of pollution, households are estimated to be responsible for around 30 percent of total environmental burdens. Encouragement of employee families to adopt less damaging practices is therefore of great importance: driving less, conserving water and energy, using alternatives to pesticides in the home and garden, using returnable containers and recycling paper, avoiding excessive packaging, and so on. Excellent popular guides, such as *Fifty Simple Things You Can Do To Save The Earth* (Earthworks Group 1991), contain handy tips easy to put into practice, and should be brought to the attention of all employees.

HUMAN RELATIONS

Experienced and successful managers know that good relations with and among employees are essential to a healthy company. The literature on human relations in industry is extensive, and we offer here only a few observations that particularly relate to the company as an environment for the people who inhabit it.

A company's internal human environment cannot be considered in isolation from its community, any more than the company's wastes or emissions. Company policies on such basic matters as wage levels, child care, and family care leave, for instance, ramify throughout a community, producing either economic stress or economic comfort in families. These have major effects on children's performance in schools and later on adults' performance at jobs, and on levels of social services that need financing by the community. If relations with employees on the job are highly combative, it is unlikely that there can exist a productive cooperation between the company and citizen groups partly made up of employees. In recent years many techniques for improving human relations and securing full cooperation between management and employees have been developed. Aside from the work-organization matters mentioned above, these include:

- Providing employee stock ownership as a means of giving employees a direct stake in the success of the company. This seems to work best when combined with employee representation in management. (In Germany, workers often have one seat on the company board of directors.) Customer and community ownership of stock might also be encouraged.

- Managing to promote cooperation rather than interpersonal competition. It has been demonstrated through hundreds of psychological experiments that people learn and perform better in cooperative situations (see Kohn 1986).

- Offering mediation processes to resolve on-the-job problems quickly, without having to resort to official grievance procedures.

- Rewarding employees (and employee teams) for useful suggestions through substantial awards of money plus public attention.

- Evaluating corporate "social performance" on equal treatment of all employees irrespective of race, sex, ethnic identity, religious preference, sexual preference, physical health, and so on. Analyze relevant company statistics on employee hiring, promotion, compensation, and other personnel-related matters. Educate all employees about problems such as sexual harassment and racial stereotyping.

- Developing cooperative working relationships with unions and regulatory agencies on such matters as health and safety.

CHECKLIST #11

TRANSPORTATION

1. Implement Antipollution and Energy-Saving Measures in the Short Term

A. Use unleaded fuel. Consider propane, natural gas, or electric propulsion for such equipment as forklifts and pickup trucks.

B. Safely dispose of used antifreeze and other hazardous substances; recycle used engine oil.

C. Consider improving maintenance and retrofit options on company vehicles.

- Keep vehicles well tuned to reduce emissions and increase energy efficiency.

- Retrofit older vehicles with improved exhaust- and noise-control devices.

- If company vehicles need air conditioner servicing, have it done by a shop with "vampire" equipment to capture CFCs.

D. Choose asbestos-free brake and clutch plates.

E. Consider purchasing retreaded tires.

F. When purchasing new vehicles,

- Inquire about energy-efficient vehicles, fitted with advanced exhaust and noise-control devices even if not legally required in your country.

- Make safety a priority: include options such as air bags, automatic seat belts, and other safety devices.

- Request information on ecological and health effects of different paints used on vehicles.

G. Support or offer partial payment for driver-efficiency courses for employees.

- ■ Recommend unaggressive driving:
    - ■ Reduces fuel use
    - ■ Reduces noise pollution
    - ■ Lessens stress for the driver

2. Reduce Unnecessary Transportation

A. Analyze travel schedules of employees in all departments.

- ■ Coordinate events to minimize travel, especially cutting down on jet travel which causes air pollution in the stratosphere.
- ■ Rely on facsimiles rather than courier services when appropriate.

B. Consider purchasing more supplies locally.

C. Consider subsidizing employees who are willing to live nearer their place of work.

3. Support Efficient Transportation

A. Plan movement of goods and components internal to the company to optimize energy efficiency.

B. Consider using electric vehicles, taking into account environmental damage caused by the generation of the electricity.

C. Provide bicycles and/or motor scooters for on-site trips.

D. Buy vans to be shared by employees who commute.

E. Reward employees who use alternative transport such as carpooling, vanpooling, mass transit.

- ■ Provide free parking in areas where parking spaces are few or costly.
- ■ Consider paying substantial sums to employees who form car pools.
- ■ Give rebates to employees who use public transit; provide company site for selling of reduced-price tickets.
- ■ Provide free shuttles to and from local public transit stations.

CHECKLIST #12

THE PHYSICAL PLANT AND ITS ENVIRONS

1. Site Selection

A. Inspect the site and official environmental data to determine what pollutants might be present.

B. Evaluate site in terms of potential "natural" risks from active geological faults, floods, radon gas, and other elements.

- If occupying site, take risks into account when planning buildings and open spaces.

C. Research regional pollution problems that might endanger employees, for example, nearby nuclear plants, oil refineries.

2. Design/Redesign Buildings for Well-Being of Users (see also Checklist #10, Workplace)

A. Take account of topography and climatic conditions in fixing ecologically efficient design.

- Position work space for efficient heating and cooling.
- Install appropriate energy-efficient window coverings.
- Upgrade insulation.

B. Plan internal organization and working procedures so that one workplace does not adversely affect another; consider, for example, noise, dust, fumes, chemicals, electromagnetic radiation.

C. Use human health and energy-economy criteria in planning heating, air-conditioning, and ventilation systems.

- Hire professional firm to conduct an initial air quality audit so that some potential problems can be eliminated by increasing fresh air flows.
- Monitor employee complaints and illness (even blood and urine samples if volunteered) to help identify so-called "sick building syndrome." Act quickly to identify and resolve interior pollution problems.

- Select windows that can be opened.
- Aim to use energy systems that allow employees to set temperatures local to their workplace.

D. Have daylight, when possible, in all workplaces, corridors, and stairways; it is preferable to artificial light.

E. Create an aesthetic workplace, giving employees a say in the decor, and providing for ethnic and cultural differences.

3. Building Materials and Interior Maintenance

A. Select interior materials that do not pose a health risk.

- Avoid new furnishings or carpets that release formaldehyde or pesticide fumes.
- Make cautious use of wood that has been impregnated with volatile preservatives.
- Favor relatively problem-free paints.

B. Remove or seal all asbestos or other similar health hazards if present.

C. Avoid using wood from depleted species, such as teak or mahogany; rely on species suited to sustainable production.

D. Choose natural local materials when possible.

E. Seek alternatives for interior pesticides, rodenticides; warn employees in advance of spraying.

F. Choose cleaning supplies that minimize or eliminate exposure to hazardous substances.

4. Transforming the Landscape

A. Design or retrofit building to respect the local landscape and nearby architecture.

B. Extend foliage areas by planting vines on trellises or walls, for shade and energy-saving as well as pleasing appearance and habitat development.

C. Reduce energy requirement for building by planting windbreaks of fast-growing trees and shrubs.

D. Increase energy efficiency by planting deciduous trees near windows that face south.

E. Warn employees if and when pesticides or herbicides are used on the grounds.

- Seek alternatives to chemicals for weed and rodent control; investigate Integrated Pest Management techniques.

F. Create a tranquil outdoor space in which employees can relax.

- Consider foot and bicycle paths, single and multiple seating accommodations, pleasing visual and fragrant surprises, wind and weather monitors, seasonally varying landscapes, and so forth. Consider ponds or fountains (with recirculated water).

G. Consider allocating vacant land for neighborhood residents to create gardens; if food plants are to be grown, check beforehand for possible contaminants.

H. Even if on a small scale, designate a portion of the site for a wild open space. Employ habitat restoration techniques in these areas. On substantial properties, hire local restorationists to reestablish appropriate indigenous ecosystems.

- Intersperse plants that supply foods, such as berries or fruits, for local wildlife.

- Sow wildflower meadow for color and nectar.

- Design special niches for animals, lizards, toads, butterflies, and other fauna.

- Create dense thickets to provide protection for wildlife.

- If appropriate, construct bird houses or nesting platforms.

- Reintroduce rare natives as specimen plants if they can be protected.

I. To reduce water consumption and gardening labor costs, use indigenous plants for landscaping.

J. If certain areas on company property are especially suited for wildlife, designate these as "habitat preserves." Such areas could include:

- Ponds
- Stream beds
- Marsh areas
- Dry washes and intermittent creeks
- Hillocks
- Rocky outcrops
- "Natural" corridors or congregation areas for insects, birds, lizards, mammals, and other fauna

K. Check site for historic or archaeological features, and make them a special point of interest.

5. Planning for On-Site Environmental Emergencies

A. Develop an environmental accident response plan (evacuation procedures, backup energy and water supply, first aid, radio and phone links, etc.) in preparation for

- Severe earthquakes
- Tornadoes, cyclones, hurricanes
- Chemical explosions
- Hazardous waste spills
- Floods
- Fires
- Toxic fume emissions

B. Educate employees about their responsibilities (and suitable safety equipment) in the event of emergencies.

C. Include neighbors in emergency planning. Educate the community about possible risks engendered by the company's operations and what they can do to protect themselves in the event of emergencies.

D. Schedule drills for different eventualities with employees and within the community.

E. Install automatic emergency monitoring and shutdown technologies for operations that involve potentially hazardous substances.

F. Provide emergency drains or catchment tanks to contain overflow effluent due to accident.

G. Install automatic alarm systems to alert employees and nearby community of accidental pollutant releases or other dangers requiring immediate response.

CHECKLIST #13

INTERNATIONAL BUSINESS RELATIONS

Environmental and social legislation functions most effectively within countries where the spirit as well as the letter of the law can be relatively well understood. By contrast, in international contexts where cultures and values diverge, the system of laws and conventions tends to break down. There is a global economy, but no simple mechanism for ensuring global responsibility. As a consequence, international business relations need special attention from an ethical standpoint.

The following Elmwood Institute principles can serve as a base for formulating international corporate goals.

- Awareness of global interdependence
- Peace and nonviolence
- Human rights
- Social and economic justice
- Personal and social responsibility
- Decentralization of economic and political power
- Cultural diversity
- Postpatriarchal consciousness
- Ecological wisdom

Social and legal conditions, economic resources, and cultural factors must be considered in developing international corporate conventions, but these should not overwhelm ecological and humanistic aims.

1. Establish Goals

A. Brainstorm ideal standards for basic environmental and social goals for overseas production sites. Various United Nations Educational and Cultural Organization (UNESCO) materials may help in defining ethical relations among disparate cultures.

B. Collect information on goods produced or consumed (in whole or in part) in foreign countries.

2. Respect the Community

A. Develop knowledge about the history and culture of foreign areas where you do business.

B. Respect the local architecture, food, language, and culture.

C. Reconsider your advertising, selling, and marketing strategies.

- Be sensitive to the problem of racial, class, ethnic, religious, or sexual stereotyping.

- Be sensitive to the problems created by introducing non-sustainable life-styles that may be disruptive to the community.

D. Respect cross-cultural differences in the way people organize and shape their relations with the biophysical environment.

3. Negotiate Standards

A. Aim to use foreign producers who apply labor and safety standards comparable to, or better than, those maintained for similar activities in the home country.

B. Write new materials, components, and labor standards into contracts with existing subcontractors.

C. Favor reliable suppliers who express a willingness to negotiate and are sympathetic to the corporate vision.

- Verify that subsidiaries and subcontractors are maintaining standards by making periodic on-site checks.

D. Develop guidelines for disinvestment or economic boycott of businesses operating in countries whose governments flagrantly disregard international environmental, civil, or social standards.

4. Implement International Standards (see also Checklist #2, Materials)

A. Ensure that goods intended for export meet or exceed the standards for protection of the environment and human health applied to comparable domestic products.

B. Aim to pay comparable, fair, and nonexploitative wages to all employees in subsidiary and subcontracted operations.

C. Avoid meddling in local politics.

D. Incorporate International Labor Organization (1988) conventions regarding wages, hazards, unionizing, race and gender discrimination into contracts; require that these be met or exceeded by firms in all signatory and nonsignatory nations.

E. Aim to eliminate categories of race, gender, ethnicity, religion, and so forth as discriminating factors in employment, promotion, compensation.

F. Do not use countries with lower legal standards as a repository for dangerous production processes or wastes.

G. Provide employees and consumers concise information on how to use, transport, store, and dispose of goods to minimize negative environmental or human health consequences.

- Provide technical training or information about products that are intrinsically dangerous.
- Label hazardous products in the language of the country of use.

H. Restrict or discontinue products if necessary for the protection of the environment or the health of the community.

5. Bioregional Considerations

A. Study applications to foreign operations of such concepts as

- Sustainability
- Biodiversity
- Appropriate Technology
- Culture

6. Resources

A. In your strategy sessions, consider whether extreme concentration of economic and political control over resources is a desirable outcome.

B. Support sustainable resource economies.

C. If you incorporate small scale crafts economies into your operations, do so in a fair manner.

7. Respect Life

A. Boycott trades (ivory, turtle shell, and other goods) that depend on endangered, threatened, or otherwise rare species, such as the elephant and walrus, green sea turtles, rhinoceros.

B. Find substitutes for goods obtained through technologies and techniques (such as drift nets) that are unnecessarily destructive to wildlife or habitat.

8. Implement More Advanced Ecological Strategies and Practices

A. Centralize information on alternative sustainable production processes in fisheries, agriculture, forestry, and so forth.

B. Stimulate markets for new sustainable technologies.

C. Communicate ecologically successful practices and technical improvements in production processes to other companies (unless economically unfeasible).

- Consider forming co-op buying groups.

D. Start a computerized network of information among ecologically conscious corporations.

E. Publicize your efforts to become ecologically and socially responsible, in your catalogue, brochure, company newsletter, annual report, and to interested environmental organizations.

11

GETTING STARTED: PRIORITIES AND ACTION PLANS

I n planning a company's approach to ecomanagement, it is not possible or desirable to do everything at once. Developing ecologically sound practices in a company will require years of consistent effort, carefully planned and put into effect with good business judgment. Here are some priority considerations that can help organize the effort. Business priorities dictate paying attention first to legal requirements, then to steps that will save the company money or increase profits, then to steps that are neutral economically, and finally to measures that may be a burden on the company or are of high risk in that connection.

ECOLOGICAL PRIORITIES

The Environmental Protection Agency (EPA) has recently rated the worst ecological problems facing the world as follows (Roberts 1990). The rank order is not of great significance.

- Global climate change
- Stratospheric ozone depletion
- Habitat alteration
- Species extinction and biodiversity loss
- Air pollutants (e.g., smog)
- Toxic air pollutants (e.g., benzene)
- Radon gas
- Indoor air pollution
- Drinking water contamination
- Occupational exposure to chemicals
- Applications of pesticides

It can be reasonably argued that company actions that may affect endangered species and the biology of large areas (e.g., rain forests) can have irreparable consequences, and should thus be first in line. (Where company activities have disturbed wildlife habitats, restoration work should be undertaken.) The elimination of CFCs is also a very high priority. Discharges that affect air quality or drinking-water aquifers also require priority attention; in some cases, indoor air quality in plants (or even offices) may present surprisingly severe risks. Possibilities of catastrophic accidents are also very high on the list for individual companies, followed by health hazards on the job or in the neighborhood of company facilities, which can have grave legal, economic, and public relations aspects. Emergency and evacuation plans, drills, and other emergency measures should be worked out and publicized (including earthquake plans in seismic areas).

The public ranks toxic waste problems at the top of its ecological worries, along with nuclear hazards, oil spills, acid rain, and other concerns. While these issues are not rated as overwhelmingly important by the EPA science committees, they do of course require attention from the industries in question.

On the next level of importance, turn to considerations of cutting water, energy, and raw material use in present processes. After that, attention can be given to process inputs: using more ecologically desirable materials. Processes themselves can then be altered by adopting different technologies or improving existing ones. Emitted substances and heat can be redirected, recycled, or reused. Once that is accomplished, residual detrimental materials (and noise) can be contained and managed for the protection needed to avoid special clothing or equipment for employees.

HUMAN RESOURCE AND ORGANIZATIONAL PRIORITIES

It is best to begin in departments of the company where employees are already interested in ecological improvements. When new staff are being hired for any department, their environmental knowledge should be taken into account. Environmental managers should be people who are qualified in ecology, business economics, and psychology. In large companies, it is unwise to set up a massive centralized bureaucracy for ecological matters; self-regulating ecological units throughout the company with some central coordination are a better ideal, but require real and lasting commitment from top management. Through proper training and motivation, all managers in the company should become ecologically minded.

HUMAN HEALTH AND PSYCHOLOGICAL PRIORITIES

From a social standpoint, first in line are health hazards, which can have grave legal, economic, and public relations impacts. For example, restrict the use of carcinogenic pesticides, consider alternatives to formaldehyde-laden new carpets in the office, and monitor any toxins which are stored, used, created, or released by the company. Good corporate citizenship requires vigilance with regard to the health of the employees and the neighboring community.

Give priority to habit-forming or example-giving steps; for example, adopting recycled toilet paper and office stationery sends a message to all who use them. Use human-interest stories to dramatize the importance of ecological measures. When steps are taken with dramatic and rapid positive effects, such as the adoption of energy-efficient lighting, make sure all employees are aware of the benefits to the company. Try to move first on matters where a consensus exists among employees, for example, the need for dust reduction; and later, on matters where there are strong divisions of opinion, for example, providing smoke-free conditions for nonsmokers in places where no public health regulations yet exist.

PLANNING THE ECO-AUDIT

As with any activity in business, careful planning is essential if eco-auditing is to be successful. It is important that the people organizing and carrying out the auditing work share an understanding of the auditing process: its objectives, its methods, and its relation to company policies and structures. This process must also be explained beforehand to the company departments that will be examined during the audit.

Experienced people in the field, including the EPA, view the audit process as an orderly series of actions and conditions, all of which are necessary if the audit is to be productive. These are summarized below. (For large companies, a written description of the auditing process is necessary, both for the auditing teams and the auditees.)

1. Definition of the Objectives and Scope of the Audit Program

Some audits, especially in the United States, have the easily defined objectives of ensuring that manufacturing units are in compliance with emission limits or other regulations. As eco-auditing objectives become broader, all aspects of a company's operation may be examined, and questions raised about company operations may seem to infringe on general management matters. Such broadening of scope is therefore probably best accomplished in stages, accompanied by ample educational work within the company. It is also important to define whether an audit is a one-time activity, or to be repeated on some regular basis, or even a continuing normal activity within the company.

Questions on the confidentiality and custody of the audit report, its distribution, and the relation of the legal department to the audit process must be settled before work begins. The auditing team should have a clear understanding of whether it is expected to make recommendations or merely state facts. A time line for the audit process must also be established.

2. Top Management Commitment to the Program

As we have emphasized earlier, if strong support is not forthcoming, the audit program will almost certainly be ineffective. Written policy statements approved at the top are one indication of support, but informal signs are equally important: being involved in top-level reporting loops, receiving frequent attention from top managers, and having problems dealt with speedily and thoroughly. The long-term success of an auditing program is closely linked to its ability to involve lower-level personnel in achieving ecological objectives. This can only happen if top management is genuinely and persistently interested. It must also be kept in mind that auditing reports that describe problems can even become a liability for a company if management does not support prompt remedies for the problems.

3. Independence of Auditors from Audited Activities

Since auditing, especially of the compliance type, may involve criticism of company people, the auditors must have independent status within the company (or as outside consultants brought into the company). To ensure objectivity, if company employees are used as auditors, they should not be expected to audit activities they formerly supervised, or currently have a connection with. Some tension between auditors and auditees is normal, as in financial auditing; but experienced auditors are skilled at avoiding a posture of blaming. They understand the auditees' point of view and help to develop a cooperative atmosphere for positive solutions that will help the company and all its component parts.

4. Proper Staffing and Training

Auditing work often demands considerable depth of technical knowledge, and a familiarity with industrial processes and practices. The auditing team chosen must possess credible competence in the required areas. If further specialized expertise is required on occasion, the auditing team should know where to find it. In companies where in-house auditing capacity is being established, staff members can join the newly developing professional associations of environmental auditors (see Appendix A), perhaps enter training programs, and develop personal contacts to take advantage of the large body of collective experience that is being built up. The level of quality in auditing work should thus rise steadily. Consultants may also be engaged periodically to help assess the auditing process.

5. Formal Audit Procedures

Auditing teams customarily prepare protocols, questionnaires, checklists, and other aids in organizing their work. This is part of the necessary planning and preparation process and must not be scanted. Much of an auditor's work is time-consuming: interviewing, checking of records, inspecting facilities, and sometimes obtaining laboratory tests. The necessary time for such work must be provided for in the audit budget.

6. Reporting

Auditing teams usually report informally on their findings during the audit "field work," sometimes verbally and sometimes through transmitting working papers to the managers involved. These serve as a basis for discussion meetings. During these discussions, misunderstandings can be corrected, solutions to problems that have been recognized may be developed, or alternative possible actions laid out. These can then be incorporated into the final report which the auditors deliver to top management; such reports often reflect a consensus on the problem involved. (More detailed material may be included in reports to facilities managers.) Sometimes responsibilities for corrections or improvements are indicated in the final report, to facilitate later follow-up checks. A closing conference based on the report is generally the conclusion of the audit process.

7. Quality Assurance

Like any business activity, the auditing itself needs scrutiny to ensure its quality. Some checks should be carried out during the process by the auditing team; some, involving the auditees, should be done not long after. Others can be done periodically. A textbook, *Environmental Auditing Quality Management* by Ann C. Smith and William A. Yodis (1989), may be helpful in the audit-planning and evaluation process.

12

CONCLUSION: THE ECOLOGICAL TRANSFORMATION OF BUSINESS

From its small beginnings, the ecological transformation of business has now become a wide and complex movement, characterized by strong currents but also eddies and backwaters. Few companies can now afford to proclaim themselves uninterested in improving their environmental performance. On the other hand, costs and risks remain to be dealt with by managers, and change in some companies seems bound to be both erratic and slow.

In the past few years, cooperation and collaboration between environmental groups and corporate managers has become much more common. Environmentalists have had to overcome their suspicions of business motives, their (often justified) fears of co-optation, and a certain lingering technophobia. While criticism back and forth will continue and even prove productive, it seems likely that we are well into a new period in which all concerned are seeking to minimize the impacts of industrial technology, wherever change is possible, rather than to assess blame or to defend the status quo.

Four areas of concern stand forth:

- The need for innovation, whether in product design or process design and operation.

- The need for responsible controls in adhering to environmental standards, whether these are subject to compliance regulations or not.

- Public information on an honest and technically reliable basis, to fulfill the public's right to know what industry's impacts are.

- Continued training and education of employees, who are essential to improving a company's environmental performance and whose health and welfare often depend on company policies.

These comprise an ethical standard for business, along the lines of the German philosopher Hans Jonas's saying: "Always act in such a way that the effects of your actions are not destructive for the future possibilities of human life."

Personal and organizational standards, however, do not always suffice. Just as child labor could not be done away with by individual companies but required nationwide prohibition by law, some environmental innovations must be instituted through government regulations that can ensure a level playing field for all companies. In case after case, industries that fought new standards on the grounds that they could not meet them have earned lasting public ridicule when they in fact found it easy to meet the standards. Sometimes, also, international competitive situations require governments to try and bring their nation's companies up to advancing international standards.

Companies that engage in thorough programs of ecomanagement have important marketing advantages as well as, often enough, reduced costs and improved profits. As we enter the twenty-first century, it seems likely that the ecological transformation of business will become ever deeper. This change will challenge the very foundations of economics as we have known it (see Figure 7 below, "Perspectives of Ecological Transformation in Industry.") New priorities will have to be defined for institutions and organizations, based on the principles of sustainability instead of exponential growth. A continual search for new strategies of change seems inevitable, in which ecomanagement will have an important role.

Fig. 7.   Perspectives of Ecological Transformation in Industry

I INDUSTRIAL SOCIETY	II SUPERINDUSTRIAL SOCIETY	III POSTINDUSTRIAL SOCIETY
Patriarchal, hierarchic top-down structures	Change and break of roles, hierarchy conflicts	Flexible, network-like models, functional leadership, synergism
Growth euphoria	Growth limits	Principle of sustainability
Quantitative fixing	"Qualitative" growth	Integrative growth
Environmental pollution	Environmental laws	Environmental restoration
Consumption of nature	Environmental compatibility tests	Creation of ecological systems
Exploitation of raw materials	Recycling, savings	Artificial "natural products"
Refuse/waste problems	"Intelligent" closed systems	Nature-integrative processes
Material basic attitude	Saturation, stagnation	Postmaterial orientation
Proletarianization	De-proletarianization	Cosmopolitan perspective
Formation of classes	Pluralism, confetti society	Virtual communities
Social laws	Welfare state	Basic securing
Product orientation	Experience orientation	Insight orientation
Mechanistic models	Cybernetic models	Systemic models
Linear idea of time	Time fractions flexibilization	Parallel time structures
Territorial expansion	Globalization, planetarism	Worldwide regionalization

Lutz (1992)

Appendix A

AUDITING RESOURCES

Several textbooks focused on compliance auditing have been prepared to raise the level of general expertise in the field. The list below
includes the most recent and authoritative works known to us, in
order of probable usefulness to most companies.

J. Ladd Greeno, Gilbert S. Hedstrom, and Maryanne DiBerto, *Environmental Auditing: Fundamentals and Techniques,*
2nd edition. Cambridge, Mass.: Arthur D. Little, Inc., 1987.

Ann C. Smith and William A. Yodis, *Environmental Auditing Quality Management.* Executive Enterprises, Inc., 22 West
21st Street, New York, N.Y. 10010-6904, 1989.

L. Lee Harrison, editor, *The McGraw-Hill Environmental
Auditing Handbook: A Guide to Corporate and Environmental
Risk Management.* New York: McGraw-Hill, 1984.

Lawrence B. Cahill, editor, *Environmental Audits,* 5th edition. Government Institutes, Inc., 966 Hungerford Drive
#24, Rockville, MD 20850, 1987.

The following organizations and institutions (in alphabetical order)
have been disseminating information and/or carrying out training
programs for auditors. Inclusion here does not signify an endorse-
ment by the Elmwood Institute.

American Institute of Environmental Property Auditing, c/o
Theodore Nearing, 1311 West 96th Street, Suite 250, Indi-
anapolis, IN 46260-1173, tel. (317) 633-4000.

Environmental Audit Forum, c/o Mr. Vinay Dighe, Occidental Petroleum, 10889 Wilshire Blvd., Suite 1160, Los Angeles, CA 90024.

Environmental Auditing Roundtable, P.O. Box 23798, L'Enfant Plaza Station, Washington, D.C. 20026-3798.

Institute of Environmental Auditing, P.O. Box 23686, L'Enfant Plaza, Washington, D.C. 20026-3686.

Institute of Environmental Sciences, 940 E. Northwest Highway, Mt. Prospect, IL 60056.

Appendix B

The CERES Principles (Formerly the Valdez Principles)

Introduction

By adopting these Principles, we publicly affirm our belief that corporations have a responsibility for the environment, and must conduct all aspects of their business as responsible stewards of the environment by operating in a manner that protects the Earth. We believe that corporations must not compromise the ability of future generations to sustain themselves.

We will update our practices constantly in light of advances in technology and new understandings in health and environmental science. In collaboration with CERES, we will promote a dynamic process to ensure that the Principles are interpreted in a way that accommodates changing technologies and environmental realities. We intend to make consistent, measurable progress in implementing these Principles and to apply them to all aspects of our operations throughout the world.

Protection of the Biosphere

We will reduce and make continual progress toward eliminating the release of any substance that may cause environmental damage to the air, water, or the Earth or its inhabitants. We will safeguard all habitats affected by our operations and will protect open spaces and wilderness, while preserving biodiversity.

Sustainable Use of Natural Resources

We will make sustainable use of renewable natural resources, such as water, soils, and forests. We will conserve nonrenewable natural resources through efficient use and careful planning.

Reduction and Disposal of Waste

We will reduce and where possible eliminate waste through source reduction and recycling. All waste will be handled and disposed of through safe and responsible methods.

Energy Conservation

We will conserve energy and improve the energy efficiency of our internal operations and of the goods and services we sell. We will make every effort to use environmentally safe and sustainable energy sources.

Risk Reduction

We will strive to minimize the environmental, health, and safety risks to our employees and the communities in which we operate through safe technologies, facilities, and operating procedures, and by being prepared for emergencies.

Safe Products and Services

We will reduce and where possible eliminate the use, manufacture, or sale of products and services that cause environmental damage or health or safety hazards. We will inform our customers of the environmental impacts of our products or services and try to correct unsafe use.

Environmental Restoration

We will promptly and responsibly correct conditions we have caused that endanger health, safety, or the environment. To the extent feasible, we will redress injuries we have caused to persons or damage we have caused to the environment and will restore the environment.

INFORMING THE PUBLIC

We will inform in a timely manner everyone who may be affected by conditions caused by our company that might endanger health, safety, or the environment. We will regularly seek advice and counsel through dialogue with persons in communities near our facilities. We will not take any action against employees for reporting dangerous incidents or conditions to management or to appropriate authorities.

MANAGEMENT COMMITMENT

We will implement these Principles and sustain a process that ensures that the Board of Directors and Chief Executive Officer are fully informed about pertinent environmental issues and are fully responsible for environmental policy. In selecting our Board of Directors, we will consider demonstrated environmental commitment as a factor.

AUDITS AND REPORTS

We will conduct an annual self-evaluation of our progress in implementing these Principles. We will support the timely creation of generally accepted environmental audit procedures. We will annually complete the CERES Report, which will be made available to the public.

DISCLAIMER

These Principles establish an environmental ethic with criteria by which investors and others can assess the environmental performance of companies. Companies that sign these Principles pledge to go voluntarily beyond the requirements of the law. These Principles are not intended to create new legal liabilities, expand existing rights or obligations, waive legal defenses, or otherwise affect the legal position of any signatory company, and are not intended to be used against a signatory in any legal proceeding, for any purpose.

This amended version of the CERES Principles was adopted by the CERES Board of Directors on April 28, 1992.

BIBLIOGRAPHY

Bauer, R. A. 1973. The state of the art of social auditing. In *Corporate social accounting,* ed. M. Dierkes and R. A. Bauer, 3–42. New York: Praeger.

Brown, L. R. 1981. *Building a sustainable society.* New York: W. W. Norton.

Brown, L. R., et al. 1990. *State of the world.* New York: W. W. Norton. (Annual publication)

Bruno, K., with J. Greer. 1992. *The Greenpeace book of greenwashing.* Washington, D.C.: Greenpeace International. (Available from Greenpeace International, 1436 U Street, NW, Washington, DC 20009)

Business Ethics. A monthly publication. (Available from Mavis Publications Inc., 1107 Hazeltine Blvd., Suite 530, Chaska, MN 55318)

Business and the Environment. (Available from Cutter Information Corporation, 37 Broadway, Arlington, MA 02174)

Butcher, J., with M. Feld. 1992. *The environmental movement: Threat or strategic opportunity?* Boston: The Boston Consulting Group.

Butcher, J., with T. Lent and A. Kleiner. 1991. *Environmental technology: Integrating the environment into business.* GBN Worldview Meeting Report, 17–18 November, Monterey, California.

Cahill, L. B., ed. 1987. *Environmental audits.* 5th ed. Rockville, Md.: Government Institutes. (Available from Government Institutes, Inc., 966 Hungerford Drive #24, Rockville, MD 20850)

Callenbach, E. 1990. *Product eco-labelling.* Global File Report #3. Berkeley, Calif.: Elmwood Institute.

Campbell, M. E., and W. M. Glenn. 1982. *Profit from pollution prevention, A guide to industrial waste reduction & recycling.* Toronto: Pollution Probe Foundation. (Available from Pollution Probe, 12 Madison Avenue, Toronto, Ontario, Canada M5R 2S1)

Capra, F. 1982. *The turning point: Science, society, and the rising culture.* New York: Simon & Schuster.

Capra, F., A. Exner, and R. Königswieser. n.d. *Changes in management—management of change: The systemic approach.* Elmwood Institute working paper. Berkeley, Calif.: Elmwood Institute.

Carson, P., and J. Moulden. 1991. *Green is gold: Business talking to business about the environmental revolution.* Toronto: HarperBusiness.

Champoux, J. E., and L. B. Goldman. 1992. Building a total quality culture. In *The nonprofit management handbook,* ed. T. D. Connors. New York: John Wiley.

Coalition for Environmentally Responsible Economics. 1990. *The 1990 CERES guide to the Valdez principles.* Cambridge, Mass.: The CERES Coalition.

Corcoran, A. W., and W. E. Leininger, Jr. 1970. Financial statements—Who needs them? *Financial Executive,* 38, no. 8 (August): 34–48.

Critical questions about new paradigm thinking. 1986. Special issue. *ReVision: The Journal of Consciousness and Change,* 9, no. 1 (Summer/Fall).

Deal, T. E., and A. A. Kennedy. 1982. *Corporate cultures: The rites and rituals of corporate life.* Reading, Mass.: Addison-Wesley.

Devall, B., and G. Sessions. 1985. *Deep ecology.* Layton, Utah: Gibbs M. Smith.

Dyllik, T. 1989. *Ökologisch bewußte Unternehmungsführung: Der Beitrag der Managementlehre.* St. Gallen, Switzerland: Swiss Association for Ecologically Conscious Management. (Available from Ö.B.U., Postfach 9, 9001 St. Gallen, Switzerland)

Earthworks Group. 1991. *Fifty simple things your business can do to save the earth.* Berkeley, Calif.: Earthworks Press.

Earthworks Group. 1989. *Fifty simple things you can do to save the earth.* Berkeley, Calif.: Earthworks Press.

Edwards, T. C. 1989. *Annotated bibliography on environmental auditing.* Unpublished manuscript, 8th ed., rev. 1. (Available from the Regulatory Innovations Staff, Office of Policy, Planning and Evaluation, U.S. Environmental Protection Agency, 401 M Street, SW, Washington, DC 20460)

Edwards, T. C. 1989. *Industrial environmental management: An annotated bibliography of practical sources.* Unpublished manuscript, 2nd ed. (Available from the Regulatory Innovations Staff, Office of Policy, Planning and Evaluation, U.S. Environmental Protection Agency, 401 M Street, SW, Washington, DC 20460)

Eisler, R. 1987. *The chalice and the blade.* San Francisco: Harper & Row.

Elkington, J. 1990. *The environmental audit: A green filter for company policies, plants, processes and products.* London: SustainAbility Ltd. and World Wide Fund for Nature. (Available from SustainAbility Ltd., 49 Princes Place, London W11 4QA, United Kingdom)

Elkington, J. 1987. *The green capitalists: Industry's search for environmental excellence.* London: Victor Gollancz.

Elkington, J., and A. Dimmock. 1992. The corporate environmentalists. *Global 500: The Quarterly Newsletter of UNEP's Global 500 Roll of Honour for Environmental Achievement,* no. 5 (April): 4–7.

Environmental Action at Smith & Hawken in 1990. 1990. Unpublished manuscript. April, updated July.

Environmental Auditor, Vol. 1, Nos. 1-3, 1989.

Environmental Management of The Body Shop International. 1990. Internal company report. July.

Fox, W. 1984. Deep ecology: A new philosophy of our time? *The Ecologist,* 14, no. 5–6.

Gabor, A. 1990. *The man who discovered quality: How W. Edwards Deming brought the quality revolution to America—The stories of Ford, Xerox, and GM.* New York: Penguin Books.

Global 500: The Quarterly Newsletter of UNEP's Global 500 Roll of Honour for Environmental Achievement. (Available from Global 500 Programme, UNEP, PO Box 30552, Nairobi, Kenya)

Global Village News. Social Venture Network, 1388 Sutter St., Ste. 1010, San Francisco, CA, 94109.

Gore, A. 1992. *Earth in the balance.* Boston: Houghton Mifflin.

Greeno, J. L., G. S. Hedstrom, and M. DiBerto. 1987. *Environmental auditing: Fundamentals and techniques.* 2nd ed. Cambridge, Mass.: Arthur D. Little.

Hackman, J. R., and G. R. Oldham. 1980. *Work redesign.* Reading, Mass.: Addison-Wesley.

Harrington, J. C. 1992. *Investing with your conscience.* New York: John Wiley.

Harrison, L. L., ed. 1984. *The McGraw-Hill environmental auditing handbook: A guide to corporate and environmental risk management.* New York: McGraw-Hill.

Henderson, H. 1981. *The politics of the solar age.* New York: Doubleday.

International Chamber of Commerce. 1988. *Environmental auditing.* Paris: ICC Publishing S.A. (Available from the International Chamber of Commerce, 38 Cours Albert 1er, 75008, Paris, France)

International Labour Office. 1988. *Summaries of international labour standards.* Geneva, Switzerland: International Labour Office.

Kohn, A. 1986. *No contest: The case against competition.* Boston: Houghton-Mifflin.

Kreikebaum, H. (Hrsg.). 1990. *Integrierter Umweltschutz, Eine Herausforderung an das Innovationsmanagement.* Wiesbaden: Betriebswirtschaftlicher Verlag Dr. Th. Gabler.

Lawler, E. E. 1969. Job design and employee motivation. *Personnel Psychology,* 22:426–435.

Leighton, T. 1992. Ten trends in corporate environmentalism. *Tomorrow: The Global Environmental Magazine,* 2,2:25–31.

Lutz, R. 1992. *Innovationsökologie.* [includes contents of this book, with much additional material]. Munich: Bonn Aktuell.

Lutz, R., ed. 1981. *Sanfte Alternativen.* Weinheim, Germany: Beltz.

Lutz, R., in collaboration with F. Capra. 1990. *The development of ecologically conscious management in Germany.* Global File Report #1. Berkeley, Calif.: Elmwood Institute.

Marlin, A. T., E. Swaab, and R. Will. 1990. *Shopping for a better world.* New York: Council on Economic Priorities.

Maturana H., and F. Varela. 1987. *The tree of knowledge.* Boston: Shambhala.

McLeod, R. G. 1990. Environmental worries affect shopping. *San Francisco Chronicle,* 3 July, Sect. A, p.4.

Mickens, E. 1991. Extending benefits to non-traditional families. *Business Ethics,* 5, no. 6 (November/December), p. 14.

Moskowitz, M., R. Levering, and M. Katz. 1993. *The 100 best companies to work for in America.* New York: Doubleday Currency.

Müller-Wenk, R. 1980. Konflikt Ökonomie: Ökologie. Heidelberg: C. F. Müller.

Naess, A. 1973. The shallow and the deep, Long-range ecology movement: A summary. *Inquiry* 16.

Oberholz, A. 1989. *Umweltorientierte Unternehmensführung, Notwendigkeit, Einführung, Erfolge.* Frankfurt: Frankfurter Allgemeine Zeitung GmbH.

Pfriem, R., ed. 1986. *Ökologische Unternehmenspolitik.* Frankfurt: Campus.

Piasecki, B., and P. Asmus. 1990. *In search of environmental excellence: Moving beyond blame.* New York: Simon & Schuster.

Pieroth, E., and L. Wicke. 1988. *Chancen der Betriebe durch Umweltschutz, Plädoyer für ein offensives, gewinnorientiertes Umweltmanagement.* Freiburg: Rudolf Haufe Verlag.

Roberts, L. 1990. Counting on science at EPA. *Science,* 249 (10 August): 616–618.

Schmidheiny, S., and Business Council for Sustainable Development. 1992. *Changing course.* Cambridge, Mass.: MIT Press.

Schreiner, M. 1988. *Umweltmanagement in 22 Lektionen.* Wiesbaden: Gabler.

Schwartz, P. 1991. *The art of the long view.* New York: Doubleday Currency.

Senge, P. M. 1990. *The fifth discipline: The art & practice of the learning organization.* New York: Doubleday Currency.

Sietz, M., and R. Michahelles. 1989. *Umwelt-Checklist für Manager.* Taunussteing: Eberhard Blottner Verlag.

Smart, B. 1992. *Beyond compliance: A new industry view of the environment.* Washington, D.C.: World Resources Institute.

Smith, A. C., and W. A. Yodis. 1989. *Environmental auditing quality management.* New York: Executive Enterprises. (Available from Executive Enterprises, Inc., 22 West 21st Street, New York, NY 10010-6904)

Steger, U. 1988. *Umweltmanagement, Erfahrungen und Instrumente einer Unweltorientierten Unternehmensstrategie.* Frankfurt: Frankfurter Allgemeine Zeitung GmbH.

Tetsuro, M. 1992. The Valdez Society research 51 companies' environmental performance. *Valdez Society News from Japan,* no. 1(October): 1–12. (Published by The Valdez Society, Tokyo)

Tibbs, H. 1992. *How many "amorys" does it take to save the world?* GBN Worldview Meeting Report. 29–31 March, Aspen, Colorado.

Tibbs, H. 1991. *Industrial ecology: An environmental agenda for industry.* Boston: Arthur D. Little.

United Nations Environment Program. 1988. *Industry and environment.* Special issues on environmental auditing, Vol. 11, no. 4 (October/November/December). (Available from the UNEP Industry and Environment Office, Tour Mirabeau, 39–43 quai André Citroën, 75739 Paris cedex 15, France)

Vaill, P. 1989. *Managing as a performing art: New ideas for a world of chaotic change.* San Francisco: Jossey-Bass.

Winter, G., et al. 1989. *Business and the environment, A handbook of industrial ecology with 22 checklists for practical use and a concrete example of the integrated system of environmentalist business management (the Winter model).* Hamburg and New York: McGraw-Hill Book Company GmbH.

Winter, G., et al. 1987. *Das umweltbewußte Unternehmen, Ein Handbuch der Betriebsökologie mit 22 Check-Listen für die Praxis.* Munich: C. H. Beck Verlag.

World Commission on Environment and Development. 1987. *Our common future.* Oxford: Oxford University Press.

INDEX

Accessibility: and product design, 110, 111; and sales strategy, 120

Acid rain, 152

Acquisition recommendations, environmental criteria for, 8

Activism, 7

Advertising: ecological, 87-89; green, 62; strategies for, 121. *See also* Eco-labeling

Advertising industry, 13

Aerodynamic products, 109

Agriculture, stimulating ecological practices in, 105

Air-conditioning systems, planning of, 141

ALVA (Society of Industry for Ecology), 57

American Institute of Environmental Property Auditing, 162

Animals, and product design, 111. *See also* Endangered species

Anthropocentricism, 61

Anti-dazzle/spatter devices, 134

Appalachia, women's co-ops in, 38

Apple Computer, 40

ASA/DIN standards, 108

Asahi Journal, 22, 56

Asbestos, replacement of, 103, 129, 139, 142

Asmus, P., 7

Assembly line, 134

Association of Young Entrepreneurs, 5-6

Associations, for environmental management, 42-57; in Brazil, 56-57; in Canada, 49-50; in Europe, 50-53; in Hong Kong, 53-54; international, 42; in Israel, 57-58; in Japan, 55-56; in South Africa, 54-55; in United States, 44-49; in Zimbabwe, 57

AT&T, 107

Auditing; expansion of, 17-24. *See also* Compliance auditing; Eco-audit; Ecological auditing; Energy auditing; Environmental auditing; Material auditing; Social auditing

Auditors, environmental, 25-26

Audubon Society, 49

Austria, associations for environmental management in, 50

Automobile industry, examples of eco-management in, 35-36

Automotive Dismantlers and Recyclers Association, 36

Autonomy, in living systems, 92

Awards programs: for employees, 78, 82, 83; for social/ecological performance, 47-48

AWIDAT (waste management information), 29

B.A.U.M (German Environmental Management Association), 13, 50

B.A.U.M. Austria, 50

BAUM Sweden, 51

Bad Brückenauer Mineralbrunnen, 36

Banks, selection of, 128

Basel, disaster in, 3

Bauer, R. A., 18

Beer brewery, ecomanagement in, 34

Ben & Jerry's Ice Cream, 7, 23, 123

"Best Available Technology" standard, 114

Bhopal, disaster in, 3, 40

Bicycling, company support for, 32, 81, 140